Lone Star Menagerie

Adventures with Texas Wildlife

Jim Harris

Republic of Texas Press
Plano, Texas

Library of Congress Cataloging-in-Publication Data

Harris, Jim, 1954-.
  Lone star menagerie : adventures with Texas wildlife / Jim Harris.
     p. cm.
  Includes bibliographical references and index.
  ISBN 1-55622-692-6 (pb)
  1. Zoology—Texas. I. Title.

  QL207 .H27 1999
  591.9764—dc21   99-051354
                                                      CIP

Republic of Texas Press is an imprint of Wordware Publishing, Inc.
No part of this book may be reproduced in any form or by
any means without permission in writing from
Wordware Publishing, Inc.

Printed in the United States of America

ISBN 1-55622-692-6
10 9 8 7 6 5 4 3 2 1
2002

All inquiries for volume purchases of this book should be addressed to
Wordware Publishing, Inc., at 2320 Los Rios Boulevard, Plano, Texas 75074.
Telephone inquiries may be made by calling:

(972) 423-0090

Contents

Acknowledgments

Writing a book is a lot of work—at least for me it was—and I could never have done it without the help of a great many people. Courtesy demands that they be mentioned, but considerations of time and space require that the list be kept to a minimum. I think I've reached a reasonable compromise here.

I had many excellent teachers in high school and college (also some really poor ones, but that's another story). I would like to thank a few of them by name, for helping me develop whatever literary skills I may have had: Sharon Conroy, Joe Graham, and Paul Lister. For encouraging me in the field of wildlife and natural history: Truman Spoon, Jim Scudday, Wayne Hanselka. Most of the aforementioned educators probably thought I wasn't paying much attention to them at the time—but guess what, I really was.

My sister, Jennifer Harris, has been my primary proofreader and constructive critic throughout my career.

My friend Tiffany Keune has been my muse and inspiration for the writing of this book; she has also been publishing and promoting my work on the Internet. Her beautiful web page (www.geocities.com/Rainforest/Canopy/1036) introduced the prototypes of several of these chapters, and will, I hope, continue to feature my natural history essays for many years to come. Next time you're surfing the Internet, stop by and take a look.

Friends who read the early drafts of book chapters and/or offered suggestions and encouragement include: Maie James, Lennie Robb, Sofia Morales, and Melinda Millar. Their kind help was greatly appreciated.

Of course, there are many more people who contributed in some way to the creation of *Lone Star Menagerie*, but listing each and every one of them here wouldn't leave any room for the book itself. Many of the anecdotes recounted within these pages couldn't have taken place without the supporting "cast of thousands" I've been running into all my life. So thanks go out to all those ranchers, wildlife biologists, cowpunchers, Border Patrol agents, hunters, illegal aliens, cedar choppers, trappers, fishermen, rodeo riders, farmers, taxidermists, game wardens, shamans, park rangers, zookeepers, cotton pickers, entomologists, trading post operators, veterinarians, prospectors, botanists, old men on front porches, and various other Texas characters who set the stage for my writings. Thanks, folks, I appreciate it.

Jim Harris
Somewhere in Texas
txnaturalist@hotmail.com

Introduction

Remember the old tale about the blind men and the elephant? One of them felt the trunk and exclaimed "Aha! An elephant is like a snake!"

"Nonsense!" said the one who was leaning against the animal's side. "An elephant is similar to a wall."

"You're both mistaken," chipped in a third. "An elephant is a sort of tree trunk." He was feeling the beast's leg. The one who had the tusk said that an elephant was like a spear, the one with the tail said it was like a rope, and the one who held the ear said it was like a fan. All of them were partly right, but all were mostly wrong.

Unfortunately, those who are totally or partially unfamiliar with the State of Texas often act a lot like those blind men. During my travels I've encountered a great many people who claim that Texas is too hot, too cold, too windy, too calm, too dry, too wet, too flat, too mountainous, too swampy, too rocky, and so on and so forth. It's actually a pretty safe bet that some part of Texas is too something for just about everybody.

The wildlife reflects this diversity. After all, what other state has both bighorn sheep and alligators? With such an embarrassment of riches from which to select, the most difficult part of creating a book like this one is deciding which animals to leave out. Naturally I couldn't include every species found in Texas; I have neither the time nor the expertise (nor, for that matter, the paper). I initially decided to limit the manuscript to twenty chapters, and then had to narrow my immense field down to twenty subjects. It wasn't an easy task, and no doubt some readers will disagree with my choices. If I happened to omit your favorite creature, well, I'm sorry (but read the book anyway; there's bound to be something in here you'll like).

I'm a naturalist, not an "official" scientist; consequently this is a book of natural history and not an "official" scientific text. Although most of what I have to say is verifiable zoological data, every now and again I've thrown in some hearsay, some history, some folklore, and the occasional tall tale. I think (hope) this is obvious wherever it occurs.

Animal writers in general tend to lean towards one of two major categories: some of us are guilty of anthropomorphism, the assigning of human characteristics to non-human creatures (the "Bambi and Thumper" school of thought). Others treat animals as though they were completely incapable of conscious thought and merely go about their daily lives like automatons, programmed solely by genetic instinct. I think I'm somewhere between the two extremes, roughly in the middle but just a hair in the direction of the anthropomorphisers. I realize that it's foolish to try to apply the full range of human emotions and moral standards to other species, but it's equally foolish to ignore them completely. Although instinct does play a major role in animal behavior, many, perhaps most, of the higher species are quite capable of feeling pain, affection, panic, anger, curiosity, pleasure; even shame and embarrassment. Anyone who claims otherwise must not have spent enough time observing them.

I should mention here that many of the situations in this book took place years ago. During much of my youth, most wildlife was either classified as game—in which case its harvest was regulated—or non-game, in which case just about anybody could do whatever they wanted with it. In today's world our attitudes toward animals have changed, and state and federal laws have been modified accordingly. Many of the things I've done in the past, such as "collecting" wildlife for pets or study, are now illegal without the proper permits. As a general rule, the public isn't supposed to meddle into the life of any wild animal—regardless of how noble one's intentions may be.

Last of all, I'm forced to admit that neither the text nor the illustrations turned out quite as well as I wanted. If I kept redoing them, they'd keep getting a little better each time; but then the book would never see daylight. I finally reached a point where I decided it was good enough to go public, but I realize that there's always room for improvement. Should *Lone Star Menagerie* appeal to enough readers, I'll do an even better job with Volume II. Let me—and the publisher—know if that idea appeals to you.

The Regions of Texas

Before we bring on the animals, I'd like to provide a brief description of the general ecological regions of the Lone Star State, broken down into geographic sections. It is, of course, foolish to pick a spot on a map and say that a certain type of natural habitat begins or ends right there, but people do it anyway, for the sake of convenience, and so did I. Also for convenience, when I divided up the map, I did it along county lines. I can't help but feel that somebody, somewhere, is going to take offense that I put their personal county in one "section" when they feel that it actually belongs in another. If so, well, I'm sorry about that.

The natural flora and fauna rarely pay attention to county lines, so they tend to overlap quite a bit. This map is intended only as a simple guideline, nothing more. (Don't try to use it to plan a road trip; it doesn't even show public restrooms.) It should also be understood that within each of the major divisions are many smaller regions, each with its own particular variations of terrain, climate, vegetation, and animal life. Trying to categorize all of them would turn this book into a whole shelf of volumes.

The Trans-Pecos

It was once commonly stated that there was no law west of the Mississippi, and no God west of the Pecos. Of course, the law moved in eventually, as it always does. As for God, I personally believe that He did some of His best work here. I'm admittedly somewhat biased in my opinion, as this is the stomping ground of my carefree youth. I roamed over much of the Trans-Pecos as a hunter and trapper (largely successful), prospector and treasure seeker (spectacularly unsuccessful), itinerant cowpuncher, farrier, horse breaker, and, finally, simply as a naturalist. I used the other occupations to make a living; I became a naturalist to make the living worthwhile.

Geographically, this is the chunk of Texas inside the boundaries of the Pecos River, the Rio Grande/Mexican border, and the New Mexico state line. From an ecological viewpoint, of course, political boundaries are meaningless lines on a piece of paper, and even rivers rarely divide an environment into distinct territories. I personally consider the eastern boundary of the Trans-Pecos to be around the area of the Monahans Sandhills.

This incredible dune land is worthy of further mention. Besides being a great place for wildlife observation and a good spot for outdoor recreation in general, this ancient seafloor hosts an extensive oak forest. These are mature, fully-grown oak trees, yet are dwarfed by the neighboring mesquites and yuccas, and even by a few stands of prickly pear cactus . . . but only above the sands. Beneath those yard-high crowns of leaf and acorn are root systems delving down as much as a hundred feet.

Much of the entire Trans-Pecos region consists of mountains, including 8,749-foot Guadalupe Peak—the highest point in Texas. (This same county, Culberson, also holds the second, third, fourth, sixth, eighth, and ninth highest points in the state!) Some geographers consider these West Texas mountains as an extension of the Rockies; others disagree. Whether or not they're the Rockies, they're definitely rocky.

Guadalupe Mountains National Park, one of the system's newer and relatively unspoiled additions, is breathtakingly beautiful. In addition to the incredible scenery, the park contains a lot of wildlife and is the only place I currently know of where all three native species of horned toad co-exist in the wild.

Precipitation throughout the Trans-Pecos is low—less than eight inches annually in some areas. Consequently, much of the area is true desert. There are some stretches so barren that the grasshoppers passing through them have to pack a sack lunch. The little rain that does fall tends to come pretty much all at once, in the summer cloudbursts, and this has gouged out "part-time riverbeds"—arroyos—across much of the landscape. Arid brush land plants—mesquite, catclaw, lechuguilla, chaparral, and lots and lots of prickly pear cactus—make up most of the vegetation in many areas. The higher elevations tend to be much richer in plant life. Some of the mountains are forested; the southernmost natural stand of Ponderosa pine in the entire world can be found in Big Bend National Park. This is another area rich in wildlife. Many animal species that are officially classified as Mexican or Central American enter the United States only in the Big Bend. It's nationally known as a hotspot for birdwatchers and is also quite popular with those who hold an interest in bats.

The Panhandle

Much of the Panhandle is one vast prairie. The early Spanish explorers named it "The Staked Plain," although I've yet to hear a satisfactory explanation why (where are the stakes?). As far as the "Plain" part of the title goes, it's entirely accurate: The best overall description of the area I've ever heard is simply that "the world don't get no flatter than this." Prior to the introduction of modern agricultural methods—and, consequently, fences and towns and such—the Llano Estecado was mile upon mile of level, featureless flatness. Great herds of buffalo and pronghorn roamed through it, packs of wolves and bands of nomadic Indians hunted them. Prairie chickens danced and procreated in the grasses, and hawks fed upon the prairie chickens. No human being actually lived there permanently, and those who passed through it had to navigate by the stars as though crossing the ocean. There were no landmarks of any sort to break the monotony.

Most of the buffalo and many of the pronghorn have been replaced by domestic cattle; a large share of the native prairie grasses have been converted to fields of grain. Windmills provide water, and highways give rapid access to the goods and services of the cities. But some hardships cannot be overcome, such as the weather. The Llano Estecado has some of the most severe climatic conditions in Texas. Intense heat in the summertime, blizzards in the winter; vicious windstorms, flash floods, tornadoes, and hailstones big enough to kill livestock.

Wildlife of the region is of the prairie variety and, although reduced in number, still reflects much of its original diversity. There are prairie dog colonies ("towns") and the associated species found along with them: rattlesnakes, burrowing owls, and badgers. Sandhill cranes, ducks, and geese migrate through seasonally. Jackrabbits and coyotes are abundant. And, as mentioned, there are still pronghorns; pronghorns like their world to be flat.

Stabbing into the eastern edge of all this flatness, however, is Palo Duro Canyon, a magnificent display of geological beauty. It's not as big as the Grand Canyon, of course, but for my money it's every bit as grand. The rugged walls of Palo Duro Canyon are ablaze with color: every possible shade, it seems, of red and pink and brown and orange, plus some black and white and a few greens and purples thrown in for variety. Cedars grow in the canyon and were once the only source of fence posts for the ranches on the plains.

During the days when Texas was still a republic, Palo Duro Canyon was unknown to the general populace and was supposedly the secret headquarters of the outlaws known as comancheros. (The story of these semi-legendary renegades was developed into an excellent novel by Paul I. Wellman and later became one of my favorite John Wayne movies.) Today the most scenic portion of the canyon is a state park and is well worth a visit.

The Central Plateau

At one time this was a shallow, tropical sea, full of armor-plated fish and Loch Ness Monster-looking reptiles. Tree-sized ferns and mosses lined its sandy shores, and pterodactyls soared overhead. Today it's a plateau, but the limestone of its ancient coral reefs, and the fossils of its long-departed sea monsters, give testimony of the past.

This is the legendary "Heart of Texas." It's a region of hills and caverns, ringtails and armadillos of what is probably the nation's densest population of deer and its largest colonies of bats. The western edges are arid semi-desert; the eastern edges are forest. At the points between, this is a land of contrast, where prickly pear cactus grow in the shade of moss-decked oak trees.

Much of the land is granite, the high-quality pinkish-gray stone from which the state capitol building was constructed (Texas, by the way, has the tallest state capitol building in the country; it's even taller than the national capitol. That took a lot of granite!). One of the many great stone masses that rise from its thin soils is the six-hundred-foot-high monolith known as Enchanted Rock—a sacred place of worship to the Comanches and probably to whoever came before them as well. There was once a plan to carve up Enchanted Rock into the Texas equivalent of Mount Rushmore, but apparently (hopefully!) it never got off the ground. Enchanted Rock has been doing fine the way it is for countless millennia and doesn't need to be carved into anything else.

Since the little bit of soil over all this granite and limestone made for poor farming in most areas, the settlers of this region were mainly livestock raisers. Cattle, sheep, and goat operations were the economic lifeblood of the region until fairly recent times. As such, most of the countryside was left pretty much "as is" instead of being plowed and cultivated. This was a boon to the native wildlife and probably accounts for today's high deer population. Deer hunting is big business now, and as long as it stays that way there will continue to be ample chunks of wildlife habitat left in place throughout the region. By accommodating the deer, landowners also accommodate many incidental species such as songbirds, ringtails, armadillos, horned toads—even coyotes, despite years of vigorous persecution by the stockmen.

Many of the larger ranches have stocked portions of their range with imported exotic species. Most of these were originally acquired for the purpose of big-game hunting, but some are kept simply for show and status. And a few (admittedly, not quite as many as there should be) are actual breeding refuges for species that are losing too much habitat or suffering from excessive hunting pressure in their homelands.

The Prairies and Cross Timbers

This part of Texas is traditionally "where the West begins." Here, the last frontiers of the Eastern Woodlands peter out into the beginnings of the Great Plains. Originally rolling prairie and oak-dotted savannahs, much of the countryside is now covered in mesquite—generated, supposedly, from undigested seeds in the manure of the vast herds of longhorns brought up from the south.

Despite the imposing presence of the Dallas-Fort Worth metroplex, a lot of the region still moves at a quiet pace, and there's plenty of wildlife around. The Texas kangaroo rat (see Chapter Eight) makes its last stand here, among the mesquite. The millions of buffalo that once roamed are mostly gone, as are the majority of the Comanches who lived off of those buffalo. But there are still deer. There are coyote, bobcat, jackrabbits, and many other small mammals. Snakes of all types are present, from tiny, harmless, worm-like species to six-foot rattlers; horned toads and other lizards abound. In the proper seasons the sky is filled with migrating waterfowl, scissor-tailed flycatchers, hawks, and doves. Dove hunting is a popular sport here, as in most of the rest of the state. The town of Olney, north of Fort

Worth, holds an annual One-Arm Dove Hunt in September, attracting amputee sportsmen from across the nation.

Near the community of Glen Rose is Dinosaur Valley State Park. There are plenty of dinosaur tracks—fossilized footprints—in the Jurassic limestone of the area. It's often claimed that these are the best-preserved dinosaur tracks found anywhere in the world. I can't swear that's true, but I can say that they're the best I've seen. The undeveloped brushy areas surrounding the sites of the prehistoric tracks serve as havens for many more modern and less glamorous creatures, such as rabbits, skunks, and quail.

Not too far from this hotbed of ancient extinction is a place dedicated to the prevention of present extinction—the world-famous Fossil Rim Wildlife Ranch. Endangered species roaming over these three thousand acres include white rhinos, cheetahs, and oryx. Most of these animals are a great deal safer, and probably better nourished, on the plains of North Texas than they would be on the African veldt or the steppes of Asia.

The city of Mineral Wells, named and famed for the allegedly medicinal waters of the area, is one of the few communities I know of where bats are treated with the respect they deserve. Bat houses on poles are a common sight (even banks have them), and the Bat World Living Museum serves as both an educational facility for the public and a rehabilitation center for sick or injured bats.

The Piney Woods

The Piney Woods of East Texas are the end (or beginning, depending on one's direction of travel) of the forests of the Southeast. Many non-Texans (and even a few West Texans, I'm afraid) are unaware of the extent of the wooded lands in this area. There are four national forests in this end of the state: the Sam Houston, the Davy Crockett, the Angelina, and the Sabine. The

Piney Woods is also home to the Alabama-Coushatta Indian Reservation, a forest-dwelling tribe, which, like many others, kept getting shuffled westward. (This was as far as they could go without giving up the woods for the prairies, and they refused to be pushed beyond it.)

The animal life of East Texas is primarily like that of the rest of the southern states: possums, flying squirrels, black bear and bobcat; snapping turtles and tree frogs; blue jays and mockingbirds. Red wolves, once common throughout the area, have largely been supplanted by coyotes but are still hanging on with the help of conservationists.

Special mention must be made of an area of the Piney Woods called the Big Thicket. It is officially known as the Biological Crossroads of North America, for this is where East and West truly do meet. In the Big Thicket can (or at least could) be found more plant species than in any other area of comparable size anywhere on the globe. Everything from tumbleweeds to bamboo is part of the natural vegetation, including over five thousand species of wildflowers. I never got the chance to explore the Big Thicket until relatively late in life so I had a lot to compare it to, and I was amazed at its resemblance to so many other ecological zones. There are parts of the Thicket that look like the Great Smoky Mountains, and parts that look like the Everglades. Certain areas could easily pass for the jungles of Southeast Asia, or the African thorn bush. One particular patch of woods I bushwhacked my way through reminded me of the Na Pali wilderness on the island of Kauai (I was almost tempted to break into a hula).

The Big Thicket has traditionally been a place of refuge—for runaway slaves, escaped convicts, hermits, draft dodgers, and renegades of every crime and complexion. It was also a refuge for the rest of God's creatures. During less enlightened days when both hunting and "development" were largely unregulated, the Big Thicket was the last haven for such hard-pressed species as alligators, snowy egrets, panthers, and red wolves. Herds of feral longhorns and mustangs were once found there, browsing on wild orchids in the deep woods. This was most likely the last haunt of the ivory-billed woodpecker (now presumed extinct) and the jaguar (no longer found in East Texas).

Much of the Big Thicket has now been converted to oilfields and pulpwood plantations. Fortunately, eighty-four thousand of the original three million acres have been saved as the Big Thicket National Preserve, about thirty miles north of Beaumont.

The Gulf Coast

Over six hundred miles of the Gulf of Mexico's coastline are in Texas. These subtropical shores are a mecca for birdwatchers, a bonanza for shell collectors, and a lucrative market for manufacturers of mosquito repellent.

The earliest known human inhabitants of this region were the Karankawas—alleged to be very tall (up to seven feet) and of a cannibalistic nature. The first recorded tourist was the Spaniard Cabeza de Vaca, shipwrecked off Galveston Island in 1528. Despite their infamous reputation, the locals didn't throw him on the grill; he lived among them for many years and became a competent herbalist and "medicine man."

The coastal marshes of Texas are the wintering grounds of many rare birds, including the whooping crane. The Aransas National Wildlife Refuge was created expressly for the protection of the "whoopers," but its fifty-five thousand acres also provide asylum for many other feathered migrants (as well as white-tailed deer, javelina, and an assortment of smaller mammals).

Not too far from the refuge is the University of Texas Marine Science Center, showcasing much of the state's impressive oceanic life. Naturally, the unwholesome side effects of civilization (oil spills, pesticide run-off, etc.) have taken their toll on the health and biodiversity of the Gulf, but there's still a great deal to be seen. Gulls, pelicans, and other seabirds are found in respectable numbers. Beachcombers can find a wide variety of colorful seashells (and, I'm told, an occasional pirate doubloon; I've never been that lucky myself). Sea turtles come ashore to lay their eggs in season, and crabs scuttle across the sands. The main hazards for barefoot strollers on the beach are stinging jellyfish and balls of tarry black residue from the offshore oil rigs.

The Gulf Coast is the main stomping grounds for the Attwater prairie chicken. This endangered bird also rates its own refuge, called, appropriately enough, the Attwater Prairie Chicken National Wildlife Refuge. During the breeding season—February to May—the booming calls of the male prairie chickens resound through the area. Their other claim to fame, in addition to the loudness of their voices, is their mating dance.

A century ago, prairie chickens occurred in unbelievable abundance, but like many another once-plentiful bird (the passenger pigeon comes to mind here), they were both reasonably tasty and fairly easy to kill. The species is making a comeback under proper management but isn't quite out of danger yet.

South Texas

Most of South Texas is another case of what was once mostly prairie now being mostly brush land. The brush was always there, of course, forming nearly impenetrable stands—bosques—along most of the riverbanks. The thorny tangles of mesquite, catclaw, and other painful prickles were originally held in check by the prairie grasses. Overgrazing of livestock gave the brush a chance to spread, and it did—beyond all expectations. The Texas longhorn evolved many of its most formidable characteristics as a result of this hostile brush land environment.

This is cattle country, the homeland of the famous King Ranch. There are still a few of the old-time longhorns around, but the locally developed Santa Gertrudis and other breeds with Brahma blood are the predominant choice for the region. The cattle share their range with a host of native species: white-tailed deer (some of the biggest in the state), javelina, coyote, armadillo, several varieties of kangaroo rat, and many other small mammals. Jaguars, ocelots, jaguarundis, and coatis wander in from Mexico every now and then. Birds of all types are abundant including a number of tropical species found nowhere else in the U.S. The Mexican burrowing toad, a tiny and colorful amphibian with a mating call that sounds like a man saying "Whoa" to his horse, also makes its only entry to our nation here.

Unfortunately, not everything that wanders up from the tropics is a welcome arrival. Most people would probably just as soon live without fire ants and killer bees, but it looks as though they're here to stay. Boll weevils weren't exactly greeted with pleasant smiles when they showed up, either (see Chapter Seventeen). The balmy climate produces a particularly pesky and ravenous breed of mosquito, and also seems to agree with scorpions, spiders, and wasps.

The warm climate of South Texas allows for outstanding citrus farming (the grapefruits here grow so big you only get nine to a dozen). It also allows a number of introduced species to thrive. Asian antelope such as the blackbuck and nilgai have adjusted to life on their new range so well that they sometimes offer serious competition to the native deer. Other exotic species—rhinos, giraffe, ostriches, zebra, and deer and antelope from every continent—are found on many of the larger ranches.

Feral hogs, the descendants of the razorback-like livestock of the early settlers, with occasional genetic infusions from wild boars introduced for hunting purposes, are found throughout much of the brush country. They still make good sport for hunters but probably have a detrimental effect on the environment as a whole. Wild hogs will eat just about anything, from a suburban flower garden to a litter of coyote pups, and their menu doesn't always agree with the balance of nature. They can also be dangerous; if you recall, a herd of wild Texas hogs almost killed Old Yeller.

CHAPTER ONE

The Texas Longhorn

I can already hear somebody complaining that they thought this was a book about wild animals, and that the Texas longhorn is nothing more than a breed of domestic cattle. Domestic cattle, you say? Could domestic cattle have crossed jagged mountain ranges and flood-swollen rivers, survived through blazing sun and drought and hailstorms and blizzards? Could domestic cattle have fought off grizzly bears and jaguars and packs of wolves; outwitted bands of hungry Comanches; bushwhacked their way through thickets of prickly pear that a rattlesnake would detour around; and grown to maturity on whatever random clumps of coarse vegetation the barren range lands offered? No namby-pamby, modern-day Angus or Hereford could have lasted a week in that environment.

I'll concede that today there are tame longhorns, which live in fenced pastures and eat commercial livestock feed; there are also tame Bengal tigers, which live in cages and eat government-inspected horse meat. Yet both the Texas longhorn and the Bengal tiger, in their natural condition, are Wild animals with a capital "W." After all, the University of Texas calls its sports teams the Longhorns, and everyone accepts that as a perfectly logical choice. But could you take these athletes seriously if they were the Holsteins, or the Guernseys, or even the Beefmasters? I don't think so.

The longhorn's exact pedigree is debatable, but some of its ancestors probably came over with Columbus. It's a fact that Spanish cattle arrived on this continent as soon as Spanish humans did. These hardy bovines were the Andalusian breed, the type still pitted against matadors in bullrings today. Barely tamed to begin with, many of them escaped into the wilderness of the New World, where they were fruitful and multiplied. Some of their progeny may have wandered into what is now Texas, although the first large-scale entry took place in the year of 1721.

A Spanish nobleman with the title of Marqués de Aguayo, having been appointed governor of Texas and Coahuila, decided to establish large-scale cattle ranching in his domain, and he had several thousand head driven up from southern Mexico. The weaker ones died en route; the survivors began to evolve into longhorns. As American settlers entered Texas, these native proto-longhorns no doubt mixed with other breeds: the predominantly English cattle of Tennessee and Kentucky and the French varieties from Louisiana. The distinctive type known as "Cherokee cattle," brought into Texas by the tribe of that name, also contributed to the longhorn's gene pool. However, most cattle historians (yes, there are such people) believe that the Texas longhorns derived primarily from the original Spanish stock.

The vast herds of wild longhorns that once roamed Texas and the Southwest were usually considered big game rather than livestock. Procuring these animals for meat and hides was more often done with a rifle than with a lariat, and bulls frequently had to be killed in self-defense. In his classic work *The Longhorns*, J. Frank Dobie tells of attacks by wild bulls upon many a lone hunter or traveler, and even on military units. Patrols of infantrymen on both sides during the Mexican war were often routed by belligerent longhorns charging out of the brush. Cavalry soldiers could be tossed in the air, horse and all, by the horns of a big bull. As the human race continued its spread into longhorn country, certain individual bulls became incorrigible man-haters and would charge without provocation. There were instances of wild longhorns attacking sleeping men around a campfire and even demolishing unoccupied cabins that smelled of their enemy. Even after the Civil War, there were plenty of dangerous cattle in the wilderness. The noted hunter R. I. Dodge wrote in 1876: "I should be doing injustice . . . did I fail to mention as game the wild cattle of Texas . . . animals miscalled tame, fifty times more dangerous to footmen than the fiercest buffalo."

And not just the bulls were dangerous; the cows were no slouch either. There's a case on record of a two-year-old heifer charging a mounted cowboy and driving one of her horns clear through the man's leg and into the horse's stomach (the rider survived; the horse didn't). The bawl of a calf in trouble would fan the fires of maternal anger in every longhorn cow within hearing range and bring them charging in looking for blood. The enemy, be it cowboy, hunter, or pack of wolves, was usually wise to retreat.

It's true that today's longhorns can be brought up to be as docile and sweet-tempered as Elsie the Cow. However, I personally believe that the choleric nature of the original beast is still just beneath the surface: When a situation calls for meanness, the longhorn has plenty of it available. By way of example, let me tell you about a certain bull I used to know....

His name was Dunk (I don't know why), and he was the rankest animal I ever attempted to ride (note the "attempted"). Just about any bull will try to hurt you if you make him angry, but Dunk was apparently *born* angry. Trying to hurt something seemed to be his primary goal in life; I think he liked fighting more than eating, drinking, even sex. Dunk would immediately pick a quarrel with whatever crossed his path: other bulls, steers, horses, humans.... I'm told he would even charge birds that landed near him and would chase badgers back to their holes.

Dunk was part Texas longhorn. He was also part Brahma, and I suspect he had come into the world accidentally: a result of a gate left open or a too-low fence between his parents. As just about anyone knows, Brahma bulls can be pretty nasty customers when peeved, but I honestly believe it was the longhorn blood that made Dunk what he was. He may have been a direct descendant of one of those man-hating bulls of the open range. If so, he did his best to uphold the heritage.

Dunk's owner had high hopes of cashing in on this extra-wide mean streak. He (the owner) wanted to make him (the bull) a star and was planning to loan him out to local amateur rodeos in order to break into the field. I had the dubious honor of making the "maiden voyage" on Dunk, but unfortunately, he wouldn't cooperate with the plan. A rodeo bull is supposed to buck and spin in an attempt to rid itself of the man on its back, and the rider is supposed to try to stay aboard through a combination of strong legs, quick wits, and good reflexes. This particular bull had different methods; he refused to buck. Regardless of flank straps, cowbells, and strategically applied cattle prods, Dunk just wouldn't buck. As soon as he came out of the chute, he began trying to rub his unwanted passenger off (and out, if possible) against the fence. If that didn't work within a couple of seconds, he'd roll over, and that *always* worked. Strong legs were no defense against this; quick wits and good reflexes might keep the rider from serious injury, but it wouldn't get him any score. This is the only instance I know about where a bull was *too* mean and *too* cunning for rodeo use.

As far as I know, nobody ever succeeded in riding Dunk for a full eight seconds, but of course Dunk never remained standing for a full eight seconds. Naturally this disqualified him from making the big time, so I suppose he eventually wound up as ground beef. And I'll bet even *that* was tough!

The most noticeable feature of the longhorn was, logically enough, its long horns. Steers grew longer horns than cows or bulls, and apparently the horns of certain individuals continued to increase in size throughout the life of the animal. There are tales of crafty old steers who managed to stay hidden in the thorn brush during many years of roundups on the open range. When finally captured (or, if too clever for that, when their bleached skulls were eventually found in some thicket) these elderly outlaws had horn spans of nine or ten feet. One of J. Frank Dobie's informants, quoted in *The Longhorns*, claimed knowledge of a Texas draft ox with horns measuring thirteen feet, six and one-half inches from tip to tip. I've personally seen living steers with horns spanning well over seven feet, and I've seen old photographs of steers with horns that possibly exceeded nine feet. The longest single horn ever officially documented (eighty-one and one-quarter inches) came from a steer of the Ankole breed, in Africa, but such records weren't kept until fairly recently. It's quite possible that some mossy-backed old Texas longhorn of the bygone days could have surpassed it. The 1998 World Grand Champion Trophy Steer, an eleven-year-old Texas longhorn named Amigo Yates, proudly sports a set of horns that stretch for eight feet, seven inches.

Mounted horns are quite another story. Museums, saloons, and tourist traps throughout the West are decorated with horns of a length that far exceeds anything found in nature. While I was in college, I had a part-time job with a company which manufactured these provincial *objets d'art*, so I speak from experience. Steamed or boiled cattle horns can temporarily be molded like clay; it's no great accomplishment to stretch one of them a couple of inches. If there is any curve in the horn (and there almost always is), it can be straightened out for even more additional length. This treatment alone can sometimes increase the natural span of a large pair of horns by close to a foot. Mount them onto the ends of a block of wood that is "slightly" wider than the skull that grew them, and you have yourself a real trophy.

The Heritage Museum in Big Spring displays a set of mounted horns spanning ten feet, six inches. This is truly impressive, even if the horns did happen to "grow" a mite during the mounting process. Naturally, nobody would ever admit to such modification, whether or not it actually happened, but keep in mind that mounted steer horns in Texas are sort of like women's figures in Hollywood—often magnificent, but not always natural.

Even disregarding its spectacular headgear, the original Texas longhorn was a breed apart. At one time it was considered a species unto itself and was officially designated as *Bos texana* (or *Bos texanus*), as opposed to *Bos taurus*, the "regular" cattle. Nowadays it's generally accepted that the Texas longhorn is a variety of *B. taurus*. There are still those who deny this, of course. There are also still those who deny that the Texas human is a variety of American. Granted, both Texas longhorn and Texas human are a bit different from the norm, but not quite enough to justify reclassification.

Old-time longhorns had several distinctive physical characteristics. The body was lean and sinewy. There was sometimes a bit of a sway in the back, and often a noticeable hump over the shoulders. (This hump, plus the thick hides and shaggy coats found on many specimens, led some observers to speculate that the longhorn was part buffalo.) The bones were dense and sturdy, the legs long, and the hooves sharp. Longhorns also tended to have longer tails than did most cattle. I can only guess at what sort of useful adaptation an extra-long tail could have been. Perhaps it was intended for swatting away extra-large flies, or for keeping at bay the vicious mosquitoes of the Gulf Coast country. (When camping out in the domain of these bloodthirsty insects, I've often wished that I had a tail myself.)

All in all, the longhorn's typical physique was an excellent one for running, fighting, and otherwise withstanding the rigors of the Texas wilderness, but not one that yielded much in the way of the choicer cuts of beef. It was said (only half in jest) that you could carry the meat from a butchered longhorn inside one of the horns, and have plenty of room left over.

Yet despite its shortcomings as truly prime eating, the Texas longhorn was the only breed of cattle capable of filling the niche in the particular time and place that it occupied. Only longhorns could have survived the hardships of the long trail drives—the extremes of climate, the frequently sparse food and water along the way, and, most of all, the incessant walking. One of the reasons that early attempts to introduce "improved" cattle in the West so often failed was that these civilized breeds couldn't handle being constantly on the move. Many generations of longhorns had grown accustomed to wandering great distances for grazing and watering; most Eastern cattle weren't up to the task. These newcomers to the open range simply walked themselves to death.

Between 1860 and 1890 an estimated ten million longhorns were driven up the trails from Texas. These drives to market were the only way a rancher could possibly make any profit, and, to reiterate, longhorns were the only cattle that could withstand the ordeal. So, had there been no longhorns, there would have been no cattle drives, therefore no cattle industry, and therefore no cowboys. This would have given an entirely different complexion to the whole panorama of what we now think of as "The Old West." Without herds of longhorns to deliver to the railheads in Kansas, there wouldn't have been any rough-and-tumble, rip-snorting cow towns like Dodge City and Abilene. Consequently, there wouldn't have been any need for tough law officers to keep the peace: Bat Masterson and Wyatt Earp would have had to find other ways to make a living. Buffalo Bill's Wild West Show would still have had Indians and buffalo, but not much else. In today's world there would be no ten-gallon hats, no rodeos, no dude ranches. Roy Rogers might have ended up a Las Vegas lounge singer, and the Cartwrights on *Bonanza* would have owned the Ponderosa Beet Plantation. Every facet of what has come to be the present-day "cowboy culture," from oversized belt buckles to steakhouses with a chuck wagon theme, owes its origin to the Texas longhorn.

Texas shaped the longhorn, but the longhorn also shaped Texas. Berta Hart Nance summed it up perfectly in her famous poem "Cattle":

> *Other states were carved or born;*
> *Texas grew from hide and horn.*
> *Other states are long or wide;*
> *Texas is a shaggy hide.*
> *Dripping blood and crumpled hair,*
> *Some gory giant flung it there,*
> *Laid the head where valleys drain,*
> *Stretched its rump along the plain.*
> *Other soil is full of stones;*
> *Texans plow up cattle bones.*
> *Herds are buried on the trail,*
> *Underneath the powdered shale,*
> *Herds that stiffened like the snow,*
> *Where the icy northers go,*
> *Other states have built their halls,*
> *Humming tunes along the walls;*
> *Texans watched the mortar stirred,*
> *While they kept the lowing herd.*
> *Stamped on Texan wall and roof*
> *Gleams the sharp and crescent hoof.*
> *High above the hum and stir,*
> *Jingle bridle-rein and spur.*
> *Other states were made or born;*
> *Texas grew from hide and horn.*

The turning of the wheels of progress eventually forced cattle ranching to become more of a business-for-profit than simply a chosen lifestyle. With such modern innovations as brush-clearing machinery, irrigated pastures, windmill-pumped water and truckloads of hay delivered on call, the cattle of Texas were no longer required to carve their own destiny from the wilderness. With each passing year, there were fewer longhorns on the (now fenced) ranges. The eaters of beef demanded softer, fattier, milder-flavored meat than the longhorn had to offer; the raisers of beef were now able to respond in kind. By the turn of the century, the animal that had literally built the West had become a rarity. Many of the surviving longhorns reverted to the wild state and became a "nuisance" to ranchers. As late as 1900, a small herd of feral longhorns in the Glass Mountains of the Big Bend region were conducting commando raids on the cattle that had replaced them on their former ranges—killing the bulls and impregnating the cows. Local cattlemen were less than pleased with the situation, and an irate rancher named Townsend eventually hunted down and shot all the Glass Mountain longhorns.

Like its predecessor the buffalo, the Texas longhorn was pulled back from the brink of extinction by a handful of dedicated men. In 1927 Will Barnes of the U.S. Forest Service collected a small breeding herd for the Wichita Mountains Wildlife Refuge. A few years later, J. Frank Dobie organized a successful campaign to maintain longhorns in Texas state parks. Thanks to the efforts of Barnes and Dobie (and their financial supporters, including many wealthy oilmen of the time), there are still longhorns in the world today.

Enterprising cattlemen eventually realized that some of the traits that make a longhorn what it is would be valuable contributions to the gene pool of modern beef animals. In addition to the well-known hardiness of the breed as a whole, longhorn cows are superior mothers to their calves. Prolific mothers, too—they often continue to produce and raise healthy offspring every season for up to twenty-five years (most other cows become barren after eight to ten years).

With these things in mind, rancher Charles Schreiner III founded the Texas Longhorn Breeders Association of America in 1964. This organization's current standards for the breed stress the good (from a modern rancher's point of view) facets of the longhorn and attempt to dilute the less desirable ones. For example, the breed guidelines look for a "mild, tractable" disposition (old Dunk would have been out of the running right from the get-go), while retaining such things as an "elliptical shaped body for heat adapting" and "strong legs with free movement." Naturally, a registered longhorn needs long horns, so a spread of at least forty inches is called for. As for coloration and markings, the association wanted today's Texas longhorns to resemble, as closely as possible, those of the trail-driving era. So, in setting down the specifications, they found it convenient to do what I have done throughout this chapter—quote from J. Frank Dobie's *The Longhorns*:

> Their colors were more varied than those of the rainbow.... There were brindles; blues—mulberry blue, ring-streaked blue, speckled blue; grullas—so-named because they had the hue of the sand-hill crane, called also mouse-colored, or slate; duns, dark, washed-out and Jersey creams—all hues of "yellow"; browns with bay points and bays with brown points; blacks, solid and splotched with white, brown and red; whites, both cleanly bright and dirty speckled; many sabinas, red-and-white peppered; reds of all shades....

There's more, but that much should convey the general idea. Just about any shade or color combination found on a cow can be found on a Texas longhorn.

When the TLBAA was formed in 1964, there were 1500 registered longhorns on the books; by 1985 there were more than

50,000. In 1998 there were over 250,000 throughout the United States and Canada. Once again, the Texas longhorn has proven itself to be a master of survival.

CHAPTER TWO

Buzzards

It's a familiar scene from many a classic motion picture. The grizzled old wagon master or handsome young cavalry scout, shading his eyes against the glaring western sun, spots a flock of buzzards circling in the distance. He knows it signifies death: a family of homesteaders massacred by Comanches, or a lone prospector who didn't make it to the waterhole in time; maybe just the remains of a feeble old buffalo brought down by wolves. It's all the same to the buzzards; it means they eat.

In many parts of the world, buzzards—or vultures, as they are more commonly known outside of the U.S.—are held in high regard for the clean-up services they provide (after all, imagine how long it would take a dead hippopotamus to decompose on its own). In parts of India and Tibet, people even use the birds to dispose of their own dead. I've always felt this was a sensible alternative to burial; personally I'd just as soon be eaten by buzzards under an open sky as by worms in a hole in the ground. Some—I could even say most—others would not agree. In 1917 ornithologist Neltje Blanchan wrote: "Our soldiers in the war with Spain tell of the final touch of horror given to the Cuban battlefields where their wounded and dead comrades fell, by the gruesome black vultures that often were the first to detect a corpse lying unseen among the tall grass." Sentiments haven't changed much to this day; vultures are still considered "gruesome."

Yes, for some reason, we Americans as a whole tend to look down on our buzzards. Granted, the biggest and rarest of our three native species, the California condor (*Gymnogyps californianus*), *is* publicly idolized. Apparently this is for no other reason than that it is big and rare. Except for that, it's just another buzzard.

The condor vacated Texas long ago, leaving behind some fossil remains as proof of previous residency, but its two smaller relations are found here in respectable numbers. Both the black

(*Coragyps atratus*) and turkey (*Cathartes aura*) buzzards still soar through Texas skies, and although massacred homesteaders, dehydrated prospectors, and even buffalo are in much shorter supply than they used to be, the buzzards manage to get along. They're not finicky eaters.

Our New World vultures and those of Africa and Asia look similar but probably aren't closely related. The prevailing evolutionary opinion is that the American varieties are descendants of an ancient stork-like creature, while those in the Old World had a type of prehistoric eagle for an ancestor. A number of anatomical differences between the two families seem to support this theory, particularly in the feet. The Old World vultures have strong, bird-of-prey type feet. Our American buzzards don't; in fact, they even have a rudimentary trace of webbing on their three forward toes—evidence of an aquatic ancestry. Hard as it is for me to picture a lake full of swimming buzzards, I suppose such things once existed. It would have made an interesting spin on the Ugly Duckling story.

By many people's standards, buzzards are indeed ugly—much uglier than any duckling could ever be. Their unattractiveness, however, is part of the key to their survival. The physical characteristics that make them so hard on the eyes are necessary adaptations to their lifestyle. (This is also the reason why the Old World and New World vulture families look so much alike; they're in the same line of work, so they've developed the same adaptations.)

The best example of this mandatory homeliness is the lack of feathers on the face and head—a concession to personal hygiene. Buzzards often find it necessary to probe deep inside a rotting carcass in order to get at the choicest tidbits. Souvenirs of this practice—clotted blood, bits of putrid meat, maggots, etc.—are much easier to wipe off of bare skin than off of feathers.

A legend common to many American Indian tribes has another explanation for the buzzard's baldness. Long ago, it seems, none of the birds had feathers; they all went around in their bare pink skins, getting sunburned in summer, shivering in the cold winter winds, and enduring the year-round taunts and snickers of the fur-clad mammals. Finally it was decided that one of the birds should go petition The Creator for some kind of bodily covering, and Buzzard got the job. (In some versions he volunteered; others have him being tricked or bullied into accepting.)

It was a long, arduous journey to visit The Creator, of course, and there wasn't much in the way of food along the route. Buzzard was forced to survive on garbage and carrion during the trip. But he eventually developed a decided taste for that sort of thing, and it became a family tradition among his descendants.

The Creator was agreeable to the bird's request to clothe their nakedness and gave Buzzard a fine selection of feathers to take back to his brethren. Buzzard made himself a somber outfit of basic black, but decided to accessorize with an impressive top-knot: huge, flowing feathers of every imaginable color. Unfortunately, he encountered some turbulent weather on the return trip and lost his beautiful headgear in a windstorm. Poor Buzzard has been bald ever since.... But every now and then, when the sun shines through the raindrops, you may catch a glimpse of the long, colorful feathers, still floating up there in the sky.

There may well be another legend behind the vulture's apparent clumsiness on the ground and its awkward hopping gait (but if there is, I've yet to hear it). The scientific explanation is that it's because buzzards are built for soaring, not walking. A vulture's flight equipment is proportionally enormous: six feet of wingspan anchored to three pounds of body. This design is what enables them to glide along on the slightest breeze or spiral upward on rising columns of warm air. An airborne buzzard is a thing of grace and beauty, despite what its face looks like in the close-ups.

The argument as to whether buzzards locate their food by sight or by smell has been going on for centuries. John J. Audobon conducted some experiments along this line prior to 1820. He first placed a fresh deer carcass in an open field, seeing if it would attract buzzards (it did). Then he placed a tanned deer hide, stuffed with straw to vaguely resemble an actual animal, in another field to see if it would attract buzzards (it did). Next he spread out a flat piece of canvas, on which he had painted a life-sized picture of a deer, in yet another field. The buzzards fell for it with no apparent hesitation, even attempting to peck out the eyes of the painting.

Field researchers have since come up with many more technically advanced and scientifically controlled versions of Audobon's experiment, but the results have always been basically the same. The generally accepted belief is that buzzards do, indeed, have a sense of smell, but it isn't nearly acute enough for them to pinpoint a dead animal from miles away, as was once assumed. Their primary method of finding food involves sharp eyesight and a lot of paying attention. When one buzzard begins to spiral down as though it's located something, every other buzzard within visual range immediately notices and hurries over to get in on the gravy train. When this happens, every buzzard within visual range of *those* buzzards joins in, and then every buzzard within... Well, you can figure out where this is going. The system works all too well, and an apparently empty sky can fill with circling vultures in an amazingly short time. This is why a buzzard will always try to eat as much as it can, as fast as it can; it knows that hungry company won't be long in coming.

I've often seen a buzzard fly a little lower for a closer look at something that might have been food, but wasn't. This is a common mistake along highways. The crafty scavengers were quick to learn that motor vehicles can be useful providers of road kill, and they scout out the areas accordingly. Sometimes the potential meal turns out to be nothing more than a discarded tire or other inedible, and the investigating vulture returns to higher altitude. However, the signal has already been detected, and others soon come to check out the tire for themselves. It's a competitive world, and no possible lead is overlooked.

In many parts of West Texas, there are miles of natural gas pipelines running through the desert. Natural gas itself is basically odorless, but for safety reasons foul-smelling compounds known as mercaptans (colloquially referred to as "skunk piss" by those in the trade) are added to it. More than one pipeline worker has told me that a gas leak in a remote section will lure in buzzards, which apparently associate the smell with a death in the neighborhood. Never having personally witnessed such an event, I can't swear that it's true. But I have smelled mercaptans, and the aroma is definitely reminiscent of something that's dead (or *ought* to be dead). I can easily believe the vultures think so also.

When nothing else is available, vultures may be driven by hunger to attack living prey. I doubt if either species would have the backbone to start trouble with anything close to its own size, but easy pickings such as insects, lizards, and nestling birds are taken on occasion. I've seen black vultures in Mexico (the same species as our Texas variety) attack newly hatched sea turtles on the beach, and I've been told by reliable witnesses that Andean condors try to push or stampede animals over cliffs. Our own buzzards have probably pulled similar tricks on occasion, but as a general rule they patiently wait for dinner to die on its own.

The turkey vulture has a red head and an ivory-colored beak, while the black vulture has a black head and a black beak with an ivory tip. The two species are often found feeding or roosting together. I've read that they will sometimes hybridize, but I've yet to come across any of these mixed offspring (as far as I know). Most likely this crossbreeding was done in captivity. Zoos and menageries have managed, in the past, to produce hybrids of a lion with a tiger, a Polar bear with a grizzly, and a bottle nosed dolphin with a pilot whale. Given this sort of track record, lighting the spark of romance between a couple of buzzards should be no great chore.

On the subject of love and procreation, buzzards probably don't look quite so ugly to other buzzards, but it still takes more than a pretty face for the male of the species to get lucky. An amorous vulture must put on a show for the object of his affections—hopping around her, stretching his huge wings, and bobbing his warty bald head. Although usually silent, the vulture even attempts to woo his lady by singing to her. It comes out mostly as harsh croaks and hissing, yet it carries all the same romantic intentions as does the song of the nightingale. Once the ice is broken with these preliminaries, the happy couple takes to the skies for the aerial portion of the courtship display. This consists mostly of soaring in tandem and wheeling around each other as they ride the spiraling air currents.

There is usually no attempt made to build a nest. If an abandoned hawk or eagle nest is located, it may be used. Otherwise, the eggs are simply laid on a convenient rock ledge, in a hollow stump, or even on the bare ground. The parents share the duties of incubating the eggs and feeding the downy white hatchlings.

A large flock of vultures roosting in a dead tree or along a line of fence posts is an impressive sight. People of a superstitious persuasion sometimes feel that a gathering of buzzards is some sort of omen of impending death in the vicinity. Actually it's no more sinister than a gathering of any other gregarious bird would be; yet nobody seems to see anything ominous about a flock of pigeons or sandhill cranes or penguins. Once again it's simply a case of bad publicity.

Buzzards frequently strike a pose with their neck and wings outstretched, looking like gargoyles on a medieval cathedral. The purpose of assuming this position is unclear; I think they may be using the fresh air and sunshine to clean their feathers. However, while doing this, they also tend to defecate on their own feet and legs. That doesn't quite fit with the hygiene theory, but I suppose this too has a valid purpose of some sort.

My own most intimate experience with buzzards happened during my teenage years, when I had high hopes of becoming one of Marlin Perkins' sidekicks on the television show *Wild Kingdom*. I figured that every animal I managed to capture would be one more line on my résumé, so I practiced my "bring-'em-back-alive" techniques on whatever I could find. At the time I was living on a remote West Texas ranch, so I had plenty of subjects available: I caught badgers and kangaroo rats; ringtails, rattlesnakes, and roadrunners; even a porcupine. There is, in fact, a way to catch a porcupine barehanded without getting quilled, but it took me several tries to master the technique. No pain, no gain.

I had a brilliant plan for nabbing one of the local turkey vultures, inspired by something I had once read in an adventure novel. I was going to lay out in the desert and pretend I was dead, and when a buzzard came to investigate, I'd grab it. What could be simpler?

In the literary version of this escapade the hero needed the foul fowl for food (he was really, *really* hungry). Of course I had no intention of eating or otherwise harming the buzzard I caught; I simply wanted to see if the ruse would work. As I had done with the other specimens I'd captured, I'd have my picture taken with it for documentation, then set it free.

The required equipment was minimal; all I had to buy was a pair of dark wrap-around sunglasses to wear during my death scene. I needed to be able to watch my subjects without them noticing that I was still alive; more importantly, I needed to protect myself. I was aware that buzzards consider the eyes of their intended meal as a sort of appetizer before the main course, and they weren't getting mine.

My staging area was near a series of cliffs where I had previously observed buzzards roosting. I arrived shortly before daybreak. (I figured that posing as a breakfast buffet would lure them in while their bellies were empty.) I managed to find a cactus-free spot big enough to sprawl out on, then there was nothing to do but lie down and wait.

It wasn't long before I was noticed. First one buzzard, then two, then four and six were circling above, apparently scrutinizing me for any signs of life. I took this as further evidence that the birds hunt by sight rather than odor; I'll admit that in those days I didn't always bathe as frequently as some people thought I should, but I don't think I smelled *dead*.

Within an hour more than a dozen buzzards had come to check me out, but I was finding it harder and harder to maintain a lifeless appearance. It's a well-known fact that we all itch the most when we can't scratch, and every square inch of my hide was screaming for my fingernails. In addition, an ant had crawled inside my ear. You'd be surprised how loud an ant's footsteps can be under those circumstances; it sounded like a team of mules walking on peanut shells.

One of the big black birds finally landed a few yards to my left and continued giving me the once-over, probably experiencing an emotional tug-of-war between hunger and caution. The others soon followed his example, dropping down by ones and twos, as more latecomers began circling above me. I had hit the buzzard jackpot and felt certain that my scheme would be a success if I could just keep still a few minutes more. I didn't move, despite the fact that the ant in my ear had invited all of its friends over for a session of clog dancing. And that a sharp-edged rock had somehow risen out of the ground and right into my back. And that the wind had filled my nostrils with the white-hot sands of the desert (and was trying to stuff in a couple of tumbleweeds for good measure). The buzzards began to shuffle-hop closer. It was working.

My plan was to suddenly come back to life and grab the nearest buzzard around the chest, my thumbs on the breastbone area and my fingers under the wings. Previous experimentation with chickens had convinced me that this was the best position to prevent injury to either the grabber or the grabbee, and I was sure that the worst that could happen was a few scratches on my hands or forearms. One of them moseyed another foot or so in my direction, craning its scrawny neck towards me, its beady eyes alert for the slightest movement. Another step, another... Target in range. I made my move, and I had myself a buzzard. Marlin Perkins would have been proud of me.

Loyalty to a comrade in trouble is not a strong point within the buzzard fraternity. The rest of the flock exploded into an every-bird-for-himself frenzy of hissing, flapping, and shoving each other out of the way, but my captive was held securely. I had him firmly in both hands, at arm's length, and was just beginning to congratulate myself on a job well done. Then I discovered what buzzards do in situations such as that one: they puke. They puke with great speed, high velocity, admirable accuracy, and unexpected volume. My earlier assumption about empty bellies had proven to be the grossest of gross conceptual errors.

As you can probably imagine, the items on a buzzard's normal bill of fare are nasty enough when they're still on its outside, and whatever time is spent on the inside does nothing to improve either the texture or the aroma. In case you're wondering, yes, I let him go. I surely did.

Although I never got the job with *Wild Kingdom*, in the years following the buzzard incident I've continued to have interesting experiences with animals throughout the world. Some of these were decidedly unpleasant, such as the time I performed a field autopsy of a decomposing walrus carcass on a remote Alaskan beach. Or the time I lost my footing in a bat cave in Trinidad and landed facedown in two feet of guano. I've found myself wearing the musk of skunks, the spit of llamas, the urine of a rhinoceros, and the snot of more than one rodeo bull. Once an elephant broke wind in my face with sufficient force to blow my hat off. But nothing has ever thoroughly disgusted me more than that buzzard I caught. In case you're wondering, no, I never tried to catch another. I surely didn't.

Horned Toads

J ust about anyplace except Texas, and sometimes even here, when you mention the horned toad, some self-appointed Guardian of the English Language will spring out of the bushes to correct you. "You mean horned lizard!" (s)he proclaims with all the fervor of the truly righteous. "It isn't really a toad." So, before this goes any further, let me explain that I know perfectly well that horned toads aren't really toads. I also know that sea horses aren't really horses, guinea pigs aren't really pigs, hot dogs aren't really... Well, maybe that one's questionable. But you get the point: They may be horned lizards in proper scientific usage, but in plain Texas English, the critters are horned toads! I've never understood why so many people seem to have a problem with this.

Of course, lizards are reptiles while toads are amphibians, and there are major differences between the two groups. Reptiles have a dry scaly skin; amphibians a wet glandular one. Reptiles give live birth or lay their eggs on land, and the offspring are basically smaller versions of their parents. Amphibians lay their eggs in water, and the young pass through a larval stage, which has gills. The similarity between a horned toad and an actual toad is purely superficial but scientifically acknowledged: The technical term for the genus—*Phrynosoma*—means "toad body."

There are several (ten to twenty-seven, depending on which reference is consulted; most experts agree on fourteen) species of horned toad, ranging from southern Canada down to Guatemala. Three of these are native to the Lone Star State: the short-horned, the round-tailed, and, of course, the Texas. The short-horned type is fairly rare in Texas, only occurring in small pockets of the westernmost areas, while the round-tailed is found primarily in the Trans-Pecos and Panhandle regions. The Texas horned toad lives throughout Texas (makes perfect sense) and is the "original" horned toad; it was the first to be scientifically documented. It also has the longest horns of the family, which is appropriate—Texas longhorns, you know—but it's not the biggest species. The regal horned toad of Arizona claims this honor, sometimes reaching seven inches in length while the Texas rarely exceeds five. Most others are much smaller, ranging between two and four inches.

Scientifically speaking, the Texas horned toad is designated as *Phrynosoma cornutum* ("toad body with horns"); the short-horned is *Phrynosoma douglassi* (it was first classified by a Mr. David Douglass); and the round-tailed is *Phrynosoma modestum* (considered "modest" because it is smaller, more timid, and less spiny than the other species). As a boy I used to classify the two common types found in my neighborhood—the round-tailed and the Texas—simply as The Little Kind and The Big Kind, respectively.

short-horned   round-tailed   Texas

Unfortunately, horned toads are much more rare today than they were only a few decades ago. My boyhood hikes through the West Texas deserts invariably turned up a horned toad or two; I rarely see any now. Overcollecting and habitat loss are partly to blame for this, but the most serious of the horned toad's problems is probably the wide use of agricultural pesticides. (Insect-eating animals get a pretty rough shake of it when all their food is poisoned.) The spread of fire ants has no doubt also had an adverse effect, as this belligerent species tends to drive away the more edible types.

This is probably a good time to mention that horned toads are now protected by law and shouldn't be captured or otherwise molested. I kept them as pets throughout my youth, but I was also willing and able to supply them with the immense quantities of live ants that they require. Most people aren't. In less enlightened times, prior to protective legislation, horned toads—living and dead—were popular souvenirs at tourist attractions throughout the Southwest. The most common of these was a highly varnished specimen mounted on a piece of similarly varnished bark or cactus wood, frequently labeled with something glib and creative such as "Howdy from Texas." Occasionally there was a little more originality. One of my most vivid childhood memories is of seeing a large display of mummified horned toads, dressed in little cowboy and Indian costumes, at a roadside gift shop. I admired the craftsmanship involved, but the overall effect was somewhat macabre.

Horned toads are completely harmless to humans. Their dagger-like spines may look vicious but can't do any real damage to anything our size. They might possibly try to bite, but even if they do, their jaws are relatively weak and they don't have any teeth. And, despite a disturbingly common misconception, they are definitely not poisonous in any way (nor will handling them cause warts).

All the different types of horned toad look pretty much alike. It's not always easy to identify the species of a particular horned toad, but the fact that it is a horned toad would be obvious even without the horns (which are, by the way, part of the skull bone and not simply an attachment). No other lizard native to this continent has the flat oval body, short tail, and fringe of pointed scales along its sides (although this last characteristic is lacking in the round-tailed variety). Coloration can vary from nearly white to nearly black but tends to be in subtle, earthy tones. Unlike some of the gaudier lizards that show themselves off with flashy colors, the horned toad's complexion is designed for camouflage. Although it can run reasonably fast (for an animal with a physique like the top half of a hamburger bun), it prefers to avoid trouble by hiding. Remaining still and flattening itself out (even more than usual), makes the little lizard seem to disappear into the ground. In loose sand, the performance becomes more than just an illusion; the horned toad can completely bury itself in a matter of seconds.

As mentioned earlier, horned toads are particularly fond of ants. In fact, when given the option, that's usually all they eat. Other prey—beetles, grasshoppers, even an occasional bee or wasp—is only taken when ants are unavailable. They swallow the ants whole, with jaws intact and presumably in perfect working order, and it doesn't seem to bother them the least little bit. However, whatever it is that protects a horned toad's inside is woefully lacking on its outside. These lizards will take up a position near an anthill and do their level best to depopulate it, until one of the inhabitants manages to sneak up behind its enemy and launch a counterattack. The reaction is one of quite obvious pain.

A typical day in the life of a horned toad begins with its head popping out of the sand or soil in which it has buried itself for the night. Like all reptiles, lizards depend on the external environment to regulate their body temperatures. After the cool of the night, a horned toad's metabolism—and consequently its movements and reactions—are somewhat sluggish. Fully exposing itself while in this impaired condition would be a good way to get eaten. As the morning sun shines upon the horned toad's head, the warming blood circulates throughout the rest of the body. When the proper temperature is reached, it's time to emerge and face the day.

The first priority, of course, is to avoid being eaten; the second is to eat somebody else. I have a theory that individual horned

toads have specific feeding areas—sometimes communally utilized—and that they are familiar with the location of ant trails
within their "home turf." At any rate, that's where I usually find
them: scarfing down ants. Feeding is done by a quick flick of the
tongue and a hasty swallow, a toad-like mannerism quite in keeping with the animal's appearance.

When not actively stuffing their faces, horned toads spend
most of their time shuttling between sunshine and shade to
maintain an optimal body temperature. Expandable ribs allow the
lizard to modify its shape for maximum or minimum heat transfer—the original solar collecting disk. Throughout the day, the
horned toad must also remain ever alert against predators. Many
other animals, from snakes to coyotes to roadrunners, consider it
a choice part of the local cuisine.

Should camouflage and evasion fail and the horned toad is
faced with the prospect of going down something's gullet, the primary back-up strategy is to make itself look as inedible as
possible. Once again the expandable ribs come in handy as the little lizard swells itself up to maximum size and shakes its horned
head like an angry bull. Sometimes it can be a mistake to try calling this bluff. I once found a dead whipsnake, its throat pierced on
both sides by the horns of its intended meal. Apparently the
snake was unable to either finish swallowing the horned toad or
to regurgitate it, and it eventually starved to death. This didn't do
the particular horned toad any good, of course, but I guess it
could be considered a moral victory for the species as a whole.

Horned toads interact with each other using stylized ges-
tures. When two of them happen to cross paths, they face off and
begin to bob their heads up and down—a typical lizard-like routine. Once the head-bobbing is completed, one of three paths of
action may be taken: neutral, friendly, or antagonistic. If neutral,
the two participants simply go their separate ways, and that's the
end of it. Sometimes they approach and lick each other in the

region of the vent, somewhat like dogs do (I don't see how this could be interpreted as anything other than friendly. *Real* friendly). If they decide to fight, which they sometimes do for no apparent reason, it can get pretty bloody; one or both combatants may be seriously hurt or even killed. I guess some subtlety in the bobbing of the heads determines the appropriate reaction, but although I've observed this behavior many times, I've yet to crack the code.

The most celebrated horned toad in the history of Texas (or anywhere else, I would imagine) was an individual known as "Old Rip." I'm neither gullible enough to say his story is true, nor cynical enough to say it isn't. My only comment will have to be that this is the way I heard it....

In the year 1897, a justice of the peace named Ernest Wood was dedicating the cornerstone of the new Eastland County courthouse. Along with the usual items sealed in cornerstones in those days—a Bible, a newspaper, a few timely photographs —Judge Wood added a large horned toad that his son had been playing with. (The man's motives for doing this are somewhat unclear to me, but I have to assume he thought it would be funny. Even keeping in mind that this was long before most people grasped such concepts as endangered species and animal rights, I still don't see any humor in the situation.)

Flash forward to 1928. The courthouse is being demolished to make way for a bigger and better one, and all the local dignitaries are on hand for the opening of the cornerstone. Old Rip's supposedly desiccated carcass is removed with the rest of the memorabilia. There, in the bright Texas sunshine and in full view of a large crowd, including city officials and members of the clergy, the horned toad awoke from his thirty-one years of suspended animation. This story may well have been the inspiration for a well-known Warner Brothers cartoon; although there is no record of Old Rip breaking into a song and dance routine upon his release.

The following year, after being exhibited throughout the country and having a private audience with President Coolidge, Old Rip passed away. His body was embalmed and put on display in the new courthouse, where he lay in state like King Tut in his golden sarcophagus. There have since been other tales of other horned toads in similar situations, but none were ever revived in front of such an august body of witnesses. Even so, most men of science take the story of Old Rip's resurrection with a large grain of salt.

Another bone of contention among naturalists for many years was whether or not horned toads can shoot blood from their eyes. Until the act was actually captured on film, many learned people wrote it off as folklore and flatly refused to believe it. I had my own doubts for a long time; I've handled horned toads by the hundred since I was a small child, and I've seen the blood-squirting trick done exactly once, when I was a college student. I was on my way to a dance on campus and was taking a shortcut through a parking lot when I spied a particularly large Texas horned toad crossing the asphalt. Never one to put my social life ahead of my reptile collection (friends called my dorm room "a zoo" for more reasons than one), I took the time to capture this magnificent specimen. While I was admiring my prize, he expressed his annoyance by ejecting a thin double stream of crimson fluid all over the front of my new white cowboy shirt.

To reiterate, that was my one and only firsthand experience with the phenomenon, although others seem to witness it on a regular basis. Some people apparently need only take a walk through the countryside and every horned toad for miles around will track them down and squirt blood on them. I guess I just don't have that gift.

I have to confess that the logic behind the process escapes me, anyway. One would assume that the ability to squirt blood from the eyes is supposed to be used for self-defense; I've even read that this will "repel predators." But is a predator with the intention of killing and eating something going to be averse to the sight of its victim's blood? That doesn't seem to make a whole lot of sense. Perhaps the key to the success of the maneuver is the element of surprise. I'll admit that it certainly surprised me!

The Ringtail

A little family background: According to the paleontologists, prehistoric North America was once inhabited by (among a great many other things) a primitive carnivorous mammal whose fossil remains have since been designated *Phlaocyon*. *Phlaocyon* was, apparently, a quite fruitful creature. Its progeny not only flourished on this continent, but crossed the ancient land bridges to colonize South America and Asia as well. The present-day remnants of this wandering family are now classified as the *Procyonids*.

Old *Phlaocyon*'s best-known and probably most successful descendant is a chubby, mischievous, bandit-masked creature that the Algonquin Indians called *arakun*—the raccoon, to speakers of plain English; *Procyon lotor* to zoologists. Despite centuries of persecution as a destroyer of corn crops and a raider of chicken coops; despite frequent attempts at extermination as a spiller of suburban trashcans and a carrier of rabies; despite being hunted for sport and trapped for its pelt (the fashionable fur coats of the 1920s and the Davy Crockett hats of the 1950s accounted for many a skinned coon), this animal has flourished. There are probably as many—maybe more—raccoons in the United States today as there were when John Smith first set foot on the shores of old Virginia.

Other Procyonids native to this hemisphere are the kinkajou, olingo, and coati. These three are mostly restricted to tropical Latin America, although there is a resident coati population in Arizona. A coati or two will occasionally wander up into South Texas as well, but they're far from common. The Asian branch of the family is represented by the panda—the red, or lesser, panda, not the more famous giant panda. Although the giant panda was long lumped in with the Procyonids, the jury's still out concerning its exact pedigree. Most authorities now believe that there must have been a bear in the woodpile.

The only other known living procyonid is the ringtail, subject of this chapter. There are actually two species of them: *Bassariscus astutus*, native to the western U.S. and northern Mexico, and its cousin *B. sumichrasti* of Central America. The two are quite similar in appearance, but *sumichrasti* has a longer tail, pointier ears, and no fur on the soles of its feet. This more southerly species isn't relevant to the book, so from here on we'll only be dealing with *astutus*.

Although "ringtail" is the usual term used here in Texas, the animal has been christened with a number of other titles as well. Some of the best known of these include cacomistle, bassarisk, American civet, and ring-tailed fox. Then there are the almost infinite "cat" names: ring-tailed cat, civet cat, raccoon cat, bandtail cat, rock cat, mountain cat, Indian cat, miner's cat, and so on and so forth. At one time it was widely believed among the less educated and more gullible elements of our population that the ringtail was, in fact, the hybrid offspring of a domestic cat and a raccoon. An interesting theory, and in some ways an understandable one, but biologically impossible. Besides, ringtails were here long before the first domestic cat was brought over.

The "miner's cat" appellation probably originated during the California Gold Rush. The ragged tents and rickety shacks of the prospectors tended to attract a lot of vermin, both human and otherwise. The pesticide of choice for the two-legged variety was a bullet or a Bowie knife; those with four legs were a bit harder to eradicate. Mice and rats infested the ramshackle dwellings like a plague, and there was no Pied Piper around to lead them off.

Ringtails eat mice and rats. True, they eat a lot of other things as well (I knew one that really loved cheese ravioli), but rodent on the hoof is always a primary staple of their diet. In fact, the ringtail's efficiency as a mouser puts the common house cat to shame, and intelligent prospectors were quick to turn this to their advantage. Enticing a ringtail or two to take up residence would not only clear out the mice, but keep down the population of spiders, scorpions, and the larger varieties of insects (also ringtail fare) as well.

House cats, due to centuries of store-bought victuals and shameless pampering, won't always catch mice. To a spoiled Tabby, mousing is nothing more than a semi-instinctive pastime, rather like playing with a ball of yarn, and has nothing to do with actual survival. Ringtails, however, are in it strictly for the food. A ringtail doesn't toy with its prey, nor does it leave little mutilated carcasses lying around for the local humans to clean up. It simply catches, kills, and eats; and it does it cleanly and quietly.

If you think this sounds like the voice of experience, you're right. I spent several chunks of my carefree youth living under conditions not too different from those of the 1849 Gold Rush. (Okay, so I had a pickup truck instead of a burro. It was still comparatively primitive.) Small rodents were frequent roommates in those days because I rarely begrudged them a little something to eat now and then; but my hospitality eventually reached its limits.

One summer I had set up housekeeping in a dilapidated trailer on a ranch in the Big Bend area. According to the Chinese Zodiac, 1972 was The Year of the Rat. I wasn't aware of this at the time, but apparently the local rodents knew all about it; the party was in full swing. That summer seemed to be their equivalent to Mardi Gras, New Year's Eve, and Spring Break, all combined into one and rolling along nonstop, with my trailer as the central staging area. I did my best to live and let live, but I drew the line when one of them chewed up a hardbound edition of *African Game Trails* for nesting material. *Nobody* messes with my library. The mice had to go.

Even in those unenlightened, pre-Earth Day times, I was opposed to using poison, so I had to rely on other means of demousing my quarters. Spring traps did no more than put a small dent in the population. Every now and again I'd get a clean shot at one of the bolder (or stupider) ones with my .22. This was psychologically satisfying but about as effective as bailing out a sinking ship with a teaspoon. I had just about resigned myself to getting some cats, even though I'm not overly fond of them, when the hand of Providence sent a pair of ringtails my way. The mouse problem was taken care of within a couple of days, and without such annoyances as litter boxes, scratching posts, and inconveniently placed hairballs. I was happy to supplement the ringtails' diet with a little ground beef or fruit cocktail once in a while to keep them in the neighborhood.

Ringtails can be found throughout much of the Lone Star State and are usually more common and more numerous than most people suspect. They're a very low-profile species, carrying on the bulk of their activities at night, quietly and elusively. They generally avoid human contact, and they don't share their raccoon cousin's penchant for mischief. "My" ringtails—the pair that helped me out with my rodent problem—eventually caught on that I wasn't going to hurt them, but they still kept their distance. I only caught brief glimpses of them, and always at night; I never did find out where they holed up during the daylight hours. The ringtail's nocturnal schedule also allows it to avoid many predators. Aside from humans (and dogs, which are usually in the service of humans), the only major threat to a ringtail is the great horned owl. It's nocturnal also and considers ringtails to be quite tasty.

As a general rule I'm opposed to making pets out of wild animals; it usually leads to no good for either the animal or the human involved. If acquired when young, however, ringtails make interesting and affectionate pets. In addition to earning their keep as mousers, the animals are simply pleasant to have around. Their lean, streamlined bodies move with an elegance and gracefulness unmatched by any other native mammal. The fur is a sort of light beige in color, whiter on the underside, with a brownish wash to it. There's a darker circle of fur around the eyes, a modest and more tasteful variation of the raccoon's mask. The eyes themselves are among the most beautiful in the animal kingdom; they have a liquid, luminous quality many an aspiring model or actress would kill for.

The ringtail is an amazingly talented climber, whether in trees, rocks, or the rafters of old buildings. The hind feet can rotate 180 degrees at the ankle, allowing the semiretractable claws to be pointed in whatever direction is most convenient. Although a ringtail's front paws are not quite as prehensile and hand-like as those of the raccoon, they can grip well enough to travel upside-down (and quite rapidly) along the wires between telephone poles. A ringtail seems to find no difficulty in running along the top line of a barbed wire fence, tightrope fashion, holding out its beautiful tail as a counterbalance.

Rock climbing is the ringtail's true forté, and it utilizes many of the same sort of mountaineering techniques favored by human climbers. For example, *B. astutus* and *H. sapiens* both have two primary methods of ascending the inside of a rock "chimney." If the passage is narrow enough, we put our backs against one wall, our four limbs against the other, and scrabble our way up. Wider chimneys can be conquered in spread-eagle position, one forelimb and one hind limb on each side. Should the span be too great to allow this method, we humans have to break out the ropes and crampons, but the ringtail has one more trick available. It springs from wall to wall, ricocheting its way up like a pinball, and makes it look easy.

As mentioned earlier, ringtails have quite handsome fur. This characteristic can often prove to be a liability; many humans feel that an attractive animal's hide would look better on them than it did on the original owner. In the ringtail's particular case, the fur doesn't transfer well; the lustrous coat of a living ringtail becomes a lax, dull pelt. It's been a couple of decades since I gave up large-scale fur trapping, and perhaps modern chemical technology has since found a way to preserve the appearance of ringtail fur; but I kind of hope not.

A prime ringtail pelt was worth about five bucks back in the mid-1970s (the last time I sold any). This was considerably less than that of a fox, raccoon, or other common Texas fur bearer—except for the possum; possum pelts went for about a dollar and a half. I never liked finding a ringtail in any of my traps; they always seemed worth much more alive and well than the five dollars one of them would bring when dead.

Ringtails enjoyed a brief popularity among trappers during the World War II era. The Office of Price Administration had set ceilings (very low ones, I understand) on pelts, and trapping was hardly worth the effort for most species. The ringtail, for some reason, was not included on the official list. Perhaps the bureaucrats in Washington were unaware that there was such an animal. At any rate, the value of ringtail pelts soon surpassed those of every other American fur bearer, and trappers were able to make enough of a profit to stay in business. Once transformed into finished merchandise, the fur was often marketed as "California mink." I suppose the naïve consumers of that generation fell for such nonsense the same way today's shoppers snap up "full-grain leatherette" briefcases and jewelry set with "genuine faux sapphires."

Although they generally go about their business quietly, ringtails are far from mute. When surprised, they make a sound something like a cross between a high-pitched bark and a whoopee cushion. A mated pair will sometimes maintain contact on their nocturnal forays with a soft kittenish mewing. They can also make a chirping sound similar to that of a raccoon. I've been told that ringtails can imitate the calls of various birds in order to lure them into eating range, but I've got my doubts about that story. This is a clever animal, true, but I don't think it's quite *that* clever.

Baby ringtails—variously known as pups, kittens, or cubs—are born during the late spring or early summer. The birthing den is usually a small cave or rock crevice, although there are known instances of hollow logs and abandoned buildings being used for this purpose. Scientific literature often states that both parents care for the young, but the only family group I've ever personally observed was a single mother with triplets. I never saw the male. (Maybe he wound up as a California mink before he got the chance to help raise his offspring.) The babies are born blind and fuzzy but begin to look like regular ringtails (in other words, get rings on their tails) at about a month old. In another month, they begin to accompany mom on short hunting trips, and in a couple of more months they're completely weaned. By winter they're on their own and by the following summer are probably parents themselves. The normal life span of a wild ringtail has never been precisely established, but a captive specimen in the San Diego Zoo lived to be fourteen.

Up until this century, ringtails were strictly Westerners. Their original range seems to have been the canyon lands from southern Oregon down into Mexico, stretching eastwards to the Texas Hill Country. Lately they've been on the move. They seem to be well established in Arkansas and Louisiana and have even been reported as far from home as Ohio. Exactly how and why this recent expansion happened is a matter of speculation, but one theory, which seems plausible, is that they take the train. Ringtails are not averse to entering barns or cabins to hunt for mice, and an open freight car would probably appear to be much the same sort of structure. If a mated pair happened to get shut inside a boxcar in Texas and were unable to get out until the door was opened in Mississippi, the chances of them catching the next train back home would be slim to none. More than likely the two would find themselves a suitable nesting site in their new territory and start doing what comes naturally: making more ringtails. Old *Phlaocyon* would be proud.

The Roadrunner

P robably no other creature, be it furred or feathered or covered in scales, is as representative of the American Southwest as *Geococcyx californius*, the roadrunner. This bird has captured the attention (and imagination) of humans for thousands of years and will no doubt continue to do so for thousands more. The roadrunner is the official state bird of New Mexico and the unofficial symbol of the rest of the region in general.

In the Pueblo culture, the roadrunner was considered a bird of great magic. Its distinctive zygodactyl feet (two toes point forward and two toes back, making a pattern like the letter X) make its tracks hard to follow; sometimes it's difficult to tell in which direction the bird was traveling. Simulated roadrunner tracks were often placed around sacred Pueblo sites in hopes of confusing any malicious spirits that might be lurking about. Roadrunners were also admired for their courage, their cockiness, and, of course, their swiftness. Eating the flesh of a roadrunner was sometimes believed to bestow these qualities upon the consumer. Roadrunner soup is still considered a general health tonic in some parts of Mexico and the Southwest today, although the custom seems to be dying out. I've heard or read claims of it being able to cure everything from cancer and tuberculosis to baldness and hemorrhoids. (As far as I know, the medicinal broth is still unavailable commercially, at least at the groceries where I shop. But some enterprising company may soon discover a vast untapped market for cans of Cream of Roadrunner or Roadrunner Noodle soup.)

Exactly how fast can a roadrunner run? Popular culture has them outrunning coyotes on rocket sleds or jet-propelled roller skates, but reality falls somewhat short of that (doesn't it always?). The only roadrunner I've ever been able to time on a straight course (a stretch of West Texas highway, in front of my pickup truck) was able to hit thirteen miles per hour, and I believe it was giving its all at the time. Of course, I had no way of knowing whether that particular specimen represented the average. He (or she; it's difficult to tell them apart without a close examination) may have been young and speedy and in prime physical condition. Or it might just as well have been old and tired....Maybe even had asthma. Even so, for a creature that size, thirteen miles per hour is a pretty good pace to maintain.

Evolutionists contend that the roadrunner is an "aberrant cuckoo"—a member of the cuckoo family, which long ago adapted to arid deserts and brush land instead of the forests preferred by most of its kinfolk. It's adapted itself well, though granted it had plenty of time in which to do it. Roadrunners have inhabited the American West for a long, long time. Their bones have been excavated from the asphalt pools at La Brea, right along with those of mastodons and other prehistoric species. Roadrunner pictures show up in ancient rock carvings and on shards of pottery found by archaeologists.

One of the predominant traits of cuckoos in general is parasitic nesting. The females of most species wait for a chance to sneak into another bird's nest and lay an egg there. The gullible "foster parents" often bust their tail feathers raising the young cuckoo, while the biological mother and father go on their merry way as swinging singles. Roadrunners, conversely, build their own nests and support their own offspring. Sometimes a small group of roadrunners will construct a communal nest and share the parental duties, but this is more the exception than the rule. A single pair will usually produce two to six offspring. Communal nests have been found with up to fifteen eggs and nestlings in various stages of development.

Roadrunner eggs tend to hatch at staggered times. It's not unusual for the oldest of the brood to be fully feathered and out of the nest while the last egg has yet to hatch. The parents continue to help their ambulatory juveniles find food until they're completely ready to run on their own two legs. This may lead to the nestlings not being fed quite as frequently as their older siblings were, and probably results in the last of the family taking a bit longer to mature.

The roadrunner, although basically a predator, is what's known as an opportunistic feeder. It can adapt its diet to whatever happens to be most plentiful at the time. This is a distinct advantage. A bird with highly specialized feeding habits is liable to become extinct should its particular prey species decline in availability; roadrunners don't have that problem. Snakes, mice, lizards, crickets, manzanita berries, baby rabbits, carrion, moths, grasshoppers, cactus fruit—all these and more are suitable roadrunner cuisine. In areas of human habitation, the birds quickly learn to exploit scraps from trashcans or leftover dog and cat food.

One of the most popular pieces of roadrunner folklore concerns their ability to kill and eat rattlesnakes. Like many of the legends of natural history, this is based on fact but tends to be overblown a bit in the telling. In my youth I frequently conducted experiments by matching together snakes and roadrunners on a level playing field to see who would come out on top; and years later I came across similar accounts, with similar results, in the book *The Roadrunner* by Norman Meinzer (see Bibliography).

Mr. Meinzer and I both found that roadrunners are somewhat hesitant to mix it up with any snake more than about two feet long. Any particularly large snakes that were encountered were avoided (sounds like a good plan to me; a bird has got to know its limitations). Usually the roadrunner would circle the snake a few times, quite literally "sizing it up," and if it looked to be too much to handle, would simply walk away.

Those serpents that were judged to be of suitable eating size were handled with the same general routine, regardless of whether or not they were venomous. The roadrunner would begin by circling the coiled snake at decreasing distances, crouching with its wings spread. Eventually the snake strikes, and the bird dodges. While the snake is uncoiled and consequently unable to strike again, the roadrunner darts in, grabs its victim by the head, and flings it into the air. The second the snake hits the ground, it's once again snatched up—by the head if possible, by the body if not—and thoroughly thrashed. The roadrunner slams the snake against the ground, against rocks, against sticks. The victim is beaten in this fashion for fifteen to twenty minutes, until it's little more than a bloody sack of broken bones. Once sufficiently tenderized, the snake is either eaten by its victor or brought back to the nest for the babies. Longer specimens are often unable to be swallowed all at once. It's not unusual to see a roadrunner going about its business with the south end of a snake hanging out of its bill while the north end is still being digested.

Two roadrunners will sometimes team up to attack a snake. Each bird follows the same basic choreography as would a single hunter, circling the prey until it strikes. Whichever of the roadrunners happens to make the initial strike follows through with the entire killing/beating/eating sequence while the other simply stands and watches. Perhaps they take turns this way, but I don't know that for a fact.

It's often said, sometimes in dead earnest, sometimes not, that roadrunners will build a barricade of cactus around a sleeping rattlesnake. Well, maybe. I personally have serious doubts about this, although I pull up short of flatly stating that it just ain't so. To begin with, I can't see the point of doing such a thing. Roadrunners are quick—more than quick enough to prevent the escape of any snake they take a fancy to—and constructing a cactus fence around it would be nothing but a waste of time. Secondly, rattlesnakes aren't exactly in the habit of falling asleep out in the open. Last of all, the whole thing just sounds like a whopper. That's my opinion and I'm sticking to it!

Prey other than snakes is subdued in the same violent way. Where horned toads and other lizards are abundant, these make up the bulk of the roadrunner's diet. Fast running species such as whiptail lizards have to be chased down, but once caught, they get beaten to a pulp also. Horned toads are treated with a bit more respect. As mentioned in Chapter Three of this book, the horned toad rarely tries to run away. When confronted by a hungry roadrunner, the prickly lizard will puff itself up to maximum size and stand as high off the ground as possible. Particularly large specimens often avoid being eaten by this bluff alone; for the smaller ones it takes a little more effort. As the roadrunner circles its prey, the horned toad turns also, maintaining a head-on position. After several minutes of this, one of the participants will give up; either the horned toad will lose confidence and try to make a break for it, or the roadrunner will lose interest and seek an easier dinner. If the lizard turns and runs, that's usually all she wrote; it will be grabbed, tossed, pounded, and eaten.

Where both the Texas horned toad (*Phrynosoma cornutum*) and the round-tailed variety (*P. modestum*) are found in the area, roadrunners show a distinct preference for the latter. This is logical; the Texas species is larger, pricklier, more aggressive, and has longer and sharper horns. All things considered, the round-tailed horned toad is both easier to subdue and requires less work to render edible, so roadrunners naturally prefer them. I suppose I would too, should the situation arise, but I hope it never comes to that.

During the early part of this century, roadrunners were not exactly held in endearment by much of the public. There was actually a bounty on them for several years. The "reasoning" behind this was that roadrunners were believed to feed on baby quail. Since most people wanted more quail around, it naturally followed that anything that reduced the quail population must be evil and should thus be wiped out as quickly as possible.

Fortunately, the roadrunner's name was largely cleared of the stigma of quail eating by a study released in 1916. Analysis of the stomach contents of several thousand California roadrunners revealed that seventy-five percent of their diet was insects, and not a trace of a baby quail was found. The price on its head was quickly rescinded, and the roadrunner is now a protected species throughout its range.

When a roadrunner's fancy turns to thoughts of procreation, the lovesick males find themselves elevated perches—a fence post, a tall mesquite bush, perhaps the roof of a conveniently parked pickup truck—and sound the mating call. This call is a pleasant cooing sound, quite similar to the noise of a mourning dove.

It takes more than a good singing voice to win the favors of a female roadrunner, however. The courting male needs to bring a gift for the object of his affections, something to demonstrate his potential as a good provider for the future family. Roadrunners can be quite particular about what constitutes an acceptable gift; some individual females seem to be harder to please than others. I've seen a female reject a number of suitors who came bearing spiders or grasshoppers, then consent to mate with one who brought her a plump horned toad. Conversely, I've also seen a female accept what was apparently the first boy to come a-callin', even though his gift was only a small beetle.

Acceptance or rejection is quite obvious, even to a human observer. The male roadrunner, gift clasped in his bill, approaches his would-be mate in short bursts of speed until he's sure she's aware of his presence. He then struts around her, wagging his tail, and begins to jump up in the air. Should the female not be interested, she simply keeps her distance, not allowing the suitor to approach her too closely. Otherwise, she will remain where she is, and one of the male's leaps into the air will eventually land him on her back. Actual copulation takes no more than a minute (running isn't all that these birds do mighty fast) and then the matter of the "gift" comes up. Often as not, the male roadrunner tries to renege on his part of the deal and swallow the offering himself. Sometimes the female manages to snatch it from him before he can get it down his gullet; usually there is a brief tug-of-war over the morsel. Whichever party wins, it doesn't seem to have any real effect on the relationship. Afterwards, the two stalk around each other for a few minutes, heads bobbing and tails wagging, then begin to preen themselves.

Although both parents play some part in the rearing of the youngsters, most of the actual nest sitting is done by the female. The male, of course, must therefore do the majority of the hunting. As the youngsters mature, both parents may leave the nest for more extended periods. Half-grown offspring accompany the adults on food-gathering expeditions to learn to hunt on their own.

Baby roadrunners have a black skin upon hatching, which gradually lightens as they mature. It's generally believed that this dark coloration is an aid to solar heat absorption, preventing the youngsters from catching a chill while waiting for their feathers to grow out. One particular patch of skin, located on the back between the wings, remains black even in adult birds. On cool mornings, roadrunners frequently raise the feathers on their backs, exposing this dark area to the sunshine, in order to warm themselves up. As most of its prey species—snakes, lizards, and larger insects—are also warming themselves up prior to emerging into the open, this schedule works to the roadrunner's advantage.

Anything as high profile and/or well liked as the roadrunner is bound to acquire a number of local nicknames. Although the roadrunner hasn't been quite as successful at this as some other creatures—the ringtail, for one example—it has still picked up quite a few. It is often referred to as the paisano (literally, "fellow countryman"), paisano bird, or paisano cock. Some people call roadrunners chaparral birds, desert chickens, desert roosters, brush chickens, or birds of paradise (I suppose that last one was coined with tongue firmly in cheek).

I once heard an anecdote of a group of New England tourists taking a discount "nature tour" through the desert. One particular member of the party was constantly complaining about everything he had supposedly come out West to experience—it was too hot, too dry, too rocky, too dusty, too thorny, etc. When a roadrunner crossed the path of the tour group, the guide pointed it out as a bird of paradise.

"That so?" commented the curmudgeonly individual. "Well, long ways from home, ain't he?"

Roadrunners are capable of producing a variety of sounds, although "beep beep" is not actually among their repertoire. One of their most common calls sounds an awful lot like a boy dragging a stick along a picket fence. Another frequent vocalization can be variously described as a buzz, a whir, or a hum (depending partly on the roadrunner and partly on who's describing it). As mentioned before, the mating call is similar to the cooing of a dove, and they can also produce a castanet-like noise by clapping their mandibles together.

Most birds are territorial to some extent. With roadrunners, the practice seems to vary among individuals. On some occasions, I've observed groups of three to ten roadrunners apparently living together in complete harmony. At other times I've witnessed a mated pair or solitary adult attack and drive off any others of their kind that ventured into the neighborhood. I suspect that the larger "communities" of roadrunners are some form of an extended family; or perhaps they're just individuals who are gregarious by choice.

Those roadrunners that do defend their territory do so with great gusto. One particularly large individual I christened "Chanticleer" had staked a claim to part of my yard (the part with the leftover dog food in it, of course). Any other roadrunner entering the area was immediately challenged. Due to Chanticleer's great size, this was usually sufficient to send them packing. If not, he had no qualms about getting physical.

Unfortunately for old Chanticleer, his personal domain included the spot where I parked my truck, so he spent a good part of each day doing battle with his own reflection in my side mirrors. He never did catch on to the situation, nor would he ever give up. I suppose he felt he'd won the war whenever the truck was gone, only to be recalled to duty upon its return to its parking place.

Chanticleer was watching when I drove away from there for the last time, moving on to new horizons. Seeing as how the truck never came back, the old bird could finally savor a lasting victory in his claim to territory. Of course, his ultimate triumph did have its downside; there would be no more leftover dog food.

CHAPTER SIX

The Coyote

Prior to the European colonization of North America, there were lots of wolves around. Wolf packs roamed over just about all of this continent, from the tundra to the tropics. However, the wolf has traditionally been one of the first casualties in every man-versus-wilderness scenario throughout recorded history, and the United States was no exception to this rule. All varieties of the wolf suffered drastic population reduction—except for the smallest species, the coyote, *Canis latrans*.

The departure of the larger wolves left an empty niche in the environment, which was quickly filled by the coyote. Once restricted to the West, coyotes can now be found across the country. Not everyone is happy about this: I once read that the first coyote seen in New England was immediately shot and its body then strung up in the town square and stoned by the populace. Although I can't verify the truth of that story, it may very well have happened. After all, with no more witches to burn at the stake, the townspeople had to do something for entertainment.

Throughout most of Anglo-Saxon tradition, the coyote is regarded as a villain of some sort. Even the name carries a stigma. Such phrases as "you low-down coyote" were standard fightin' words in many a B-Western. Today "coyote" is the borderland term for a smuggler of illegal aliens, who is usually not a particularly nice sort of fellow. (Most two-legged "coyotes" bleed their clients for everything they own, then sneak them into the country under conditions not much removed from the days of the African slave trade. Just recently a Border Patrol checkpoint discovered a rental trailer so stuffed with illegals that a woman in the center had died of suffocation.)

Cartoon coyotes spend their days trying to kill cute, lovable roadrunners. Flesh-and-blood coyotes frequently receive the blame for every sheep, goat, and calf that expires on the range, regardless of the actual cause of death. There is rarely a closed season on the coyote, and in many areas there are still bounties on them.

Native American opinion of the little wolf was much higher. In many Indian legends, Coyote was the creator of Man, or at the very least, a major benefactor (supplying the human race with fire, teaching us how to plant corn, etc.). Not that he didn't have his less lovable side. He was frequently given to playing cruel practical jokes on other creatures.

Cattlemen and coyotes never had too much trouble with each other in the early days of the West and co-existed in a mostly peaceable fashion. In fact, coyotes are actually something of a boon to the range cattle industry, as they prey on other grass-eaters that would otherwise compete with the cows. Once sheep moved in, however, everything changed, and large-scale extermination of the coyote was attempted. Between 1919 and 1946, agents of the U.S. Fish and Wildlife Service killed over a million and a half coyotes. Fur trappers, bounty hunters, sportsmen, and irate sheepherders may have taken that many as well. Yet the coyote continues to increase in numbers and expand its range, and I've got to admire it for that.

Do coyotes actually kill sheep? Well, of course they do (although not to the extent that many sheep ranchers would have you believe). The coyote is, after all, a wolf, and wolves are predators. Predators kill to eat, and eating frequently depends on locating easy prey. Sheep, by their gregarious nature, astounding lack of survival skills, and outright stupidity, are pretty much the pinnacle of easy prey.

I can't prove it, but my personal opinion is that coyotes often consider sheep to be a last resort. During my lifetime I've examined the stomach contents of hundreds of coyotes and found that mutton and lamb do not appear on the menu nearly as often as would be expected. The main staple of a coyote's diet is rodents—pack rats, field mice, kangaroo rats. Rabbits are another popular item, as are insects and lizards. Fawns of both deer and pronghorn may be taken, and perhaps adults of these animals if they can be found in a weakened condition. Coyotes also eat a lot more vegetable matter than do most other canines (in fact, they're extremely fond of watermelon). A coyote will eat nestling birds and eggs, juniper berries, horned toads, mesquite beans, fish, garbage, and carrion. This last habit accounts for much of their bad reputation. Any livestock that dies in coyote country is going to be eaten by coyotes. Regardless of whether the animal freezes to death, gets struck by lightning, or dies of a broken heart, its carcass will be found surrounded by coyote tracks. As a result of this, the coyotes will most likely be charged with the actual killing—guilt by association, so to speak.

It's not the usual situation, but sometimes coyotes become sheep killers on a regular basis. A certain pair of West Texas coyotes had developed the habit of killing and mutilating every sheep they could find and not even eating most of the carcasses. I have no idea why they did this. They seemed to be in perfect physical condition, and there was sufficient natural prey in the area to support them. All I can theorize is that some coyotes, like some humans, are simply twisted sadists that find pleasure in victimizing weaker creatures. I can't explain how individuals of either species come to be that way.

The local stockmen were planning to retaliate against these two individual coyotes by slathering most of the range land in the county with a variety of deadly poisons, thus contaminating the food chain for years to come and probably wiping out thousands of innocent animals from kangaroo rats to butterflies. Unfortunately, this was a pretty standard reaction in much of the West only a few decades ago, but a few of the more clear-thinking ranchers managed to get a postponement of thirty days to see if someone could seek out and destroy the sheep-killers. As it happened, I was the one who found and killed them. I took no particular pleasure in their deaths; if the truth be known, I like coyotes much better than I like sheep. The demise of two coyotes was, however, a preferred alternative to wholesale toxification of the countryside.

Unlike sheep, cattle actually have little to fear from coyotes. It's possible that a pair of coyotes may try to take on a cow in labor, a very young calf, or a sick or injured adult steer, although this is unusual. Coyotes do tend to hang around herds of cattle during the calving season, but their main goal is scavenging the afterbirth. Some individual coyotes develop the habit of "tail-cropping"; they will eat the tails off very young calves. Oddly, the calves in question often show no concern about the operation or even seem to take any notice of it happening. But nobody ever said calves were overly bright.

When the famous San Diego Zoo expanded its operations with the construction of the Wild Animal Park, coyotes became a factor. When hundreds of acres of rural Southern California were suddenly stocked with free-roaming wild game, the local coyotes knew a good thing when they saw it. Many of the animals introduced—giraffes and rhinos, for example—were far beyond the coyotes' maximum size limit for acceptable prey. Others were not—most of the birds, for example. It had been the intentions of the designers to allow such exotic avifauna as flamingos, storks, and rare pheasants to roam about freely, but to keep them from flying off the grounds, most were pinioned. To a coyote, a large flightless bird, confined in an enclosed area, is basically a bucket of chicken.

"Coyote-proof" fencing (actually, there's no such thing—better fences may keep the coyotes out for a while longer, but will eventually be breached) was installed. Unfortunately, with the coyotes temporarily absent, the rodent population mushroomed. Besides being safe from their normal predator, the rats and mice were gorging themselves on feed left out for the exotic livestock.

Eventually the coyotes got back in, as most people knew they would, but by this time an acceptable balance had been worked out. The pinioned birds were housed in special enclosures to keep them out of harm's way. Native rodents were held to normal levels through coyote predation. Occasionally a baby of one of the smaller antelope species would be taken by coyotes as well, but losses were not serious enough to outweigh a previously overlooked benefit—natural defense behavior. One of the goals of the San Diego Wild Animal Park is to build up sufficient reserves of certain creatures to repopulate their native habitats if need be. Hoofed game raised in a totally predator-free environment would be unable to survive if suddenly returned to a wild, tooth-and-claw neighborhood. Coyotes are dangerous enough to keep the animals on their toes, so to speak, while not so dangerous as to be an actual threat to their survival. So, you see, the story does have a happy ending.

The coyote is, in many ways, a wolf that never quite grew up. In addition to being of a smaller size than their brethren, coyotes maintain a juvenile playfulness that the larger wolves seem to consider beneath the dignity of their station. Observations of coyotes consistently reveal much more "play" activity than is normally seen among timber wolves. This may be due in part to the differences in social structure between the two species. Coyotes rarely form organized "packs." Although sometimes found in close association with others of their kind, they mostly prefer to live alone or in couples. When larger groups are seen, they usually consist of a mated pair and their nearly grown offspring.

Timber wolves, on the other hand, often form well-organized bands in which good order and discipline are essential. The coyote's *joie de vivre* and occasional bursts of silliness would be unable to fit into such a lifestyle. Unfortunately, the pack instinct is another one of the reasons that the timber wolf has suffered much greater casualties from humans. It's easier to locate and destroy a large group than a scattering of individuals.

Pecos Bill, the ultimate figure in Texas folklore, was raised by coyotes. Even after his integration into human society, Bill largely retained his position as the coyotes' leader, much as Tarzan remained King of the Apes while simultaneously serving as Lord Greystoke in England.

On the day of Pecos Bill's scheduled marriage to Slue-Foot Sue, the stubborn bride-to-be attempted to ride Bill's horse Widowmaker. She was thrown, of course, and due to the fact that she wore a springy bustle under her wedding gown, she bounced—all the way up to the moon, in fact; and there she stayed. In despair over the loss of his beloved, Pecos Bill spent every night for the rest of his life howling sadly at the moon. His loyal coyote subjects did the same, out of sympathy.

That's one explanation as to why coyotes howl, but modern-day zoologists have come up with other theories. The most frequent reason why coyotes (and wolves, and domestic dogs) howl is simply to announce their presence to the world—to say "Here I am!" Subtle nuances in the howling may be used to indicate specific details. Howling can be a means of claiming specific territory, of looking for a mate, or of keeping tabs on the position of a hunting partner. A howl can also be an expression of frustration (easily demonstrated with any species of canine). If a male is within scent range of a female in heat but unable to get to her, he will howl. And howl. And howl.

One howl will lead to another. A noise even remotely resembling a howl will elicit an answer from any coyotes in the vicinity. I've heard them respond to sirens, car horns, and my own attempts at imitating them. My companion of many years, a dog/coyote hybrid named Cholla, would consistently begin to howl at certain musical passages. I once spent several long winter nights testing her reaction to my cassette library. I found that she always felt obliged to "answer" Eddy Arnold singing "Cattle Call" or the Sons of the Pioneers performing their rendition of "Cool Water." Certain other songs would also catch her attention, but these were her clear favorites.

Much has been written about the coyote's "psychic" ability to detect danger. I'm not such a skeptic to say that such a thing does not exist, but I believe a lot of it can be explained in a more rational fashion. To begin with, all canines—and possibly coyotes in particular—have an extremely well developed sense of smell. Our own species relies primarily on sight and sound to gather information on our surroundings, and we may tend to forget that other creatures do things differently. In a coyote's world, odors that are completely undetectable to us are as plain as neon signs.

One outstanding example is the fact that I come across wild coyotes much more often when I'm not carrying a gun. There's nothing the least bit metaphysical about this. Firearms have a distinctive odor that animals can detect from quite a distance, and coyotes are intelligent enough to realize the implications. If a coyote happens to smell me, its reaction is something along the lines of "a human—better be sort of cautious." If it smells my gun, the signal changes to "an armed human—feet, don't fail me now!" Cholla knew perfectly well what a gun was for and even understood which end of it was the dangerous one. In another controlled experiment with her, I would handle unloaded firearms so that I happened to "casually" point them in her direction, and she always "casually" moved out of the way. Regardless of whether she was standing, sitting, or lying down; regardless of whether she seemed to be paying attention at the time; regardless of whether it was rifle, pistol, or shotgun, she always removed herself from the line of fire. I'm sure she realized I would never deliberately shoot her, but she wasn't about to take any chances of a mishap occurring. Most humans should be so smart.

Coyotes are also often credited with "knowing" whether or not an animal carcass has been poisoned and left out as bait. Besides their ability to smell and, therefore, reject many types of poison, the little wolves are simply cautious. Coyotes are often the first to find any carrion in the area, but if there is the least bit of suspicion, they'll be the last to sample it. They frequently wait and watch while other, more trusting scavengers take the initiative. If nothing seems amiss, the coyotes then move in.

The language of odors plays a much larger part in the coyote's life than just warning of danger, of course. Throughout the canine family, scent-marking is an important activity. All species of dog can both send and receive quite complex messages through their bodily wastes. A good sniff of dried urine can reveal a great deal about the "owner"—age, gender, sexual status, and possibly a number of other things humans don't even suspect. Feces, too, are important indicators. The coyote has a pair of scent glands in the anal region that transfer the individual's signature aroma to every one of nature's little packages it leaves behind, and these are thoroughly investigated by other coyotes that come across them. I've yet to meet a man who could identify his own—or any other—dog by a whiff of the animal's droppings, but it's no great task for another canine. When your family pooch noses around a pile of feces, it's simply checking where it came from: "Why, it's old Rover; guess he's back from the boarding kennel," or "Hey, I don't know this guy; must be new in the neighborhood."

Coyotes, like domestic dogs, frequently roll in any strong-smelling substances they find—livestock dung, dead fish, rancid garbage, etc. There are several theories as to why they do this, the most logical being that they're trying to disguise their own aroma to fool their prey. Other animals rely on warning odors also, and such species as rabbits are less likely to be spooked by the smell of a cow patty than the smell of a coyote. This may be true, but I have my own opinion as to why dogs and coyotes roll in rank substances. I think they simply enjoy doing it. Watch a dog's face when it's wallowing in something that really stinks, and tell me that's not an expression of ecstasy.

Mating season for the coyote usually occurs in the January to April time frame, and the pups are born about two months later. Litters as large as fourteen have been reported, but the average is five or six. (The biggest litter I've ever personally seen contained eight pups, but one of them, a sickly-looking runt, died within a week of birth.) In an area with a dense coyote population, litters tend to be smaller than average, and the reverse is also true. When there's plenty of territory available, the litters are bigger. The preferred den site is a rock crevice on a brushy slope. However, the coyote's taste in housing is almost as opportunistic as its taste in food—most anything will do in a pinch. Coyotes have been found rearing their litters in everything from hollow logs to badger holes to empty oil drums. Females who have located a premium den within their home territory often use it year after year.

Although the coyote isn't a strictly monogamous species, long-term relationships are the rule. A mated pair usually spends most of its time together. When the female is giving birth or nursing the newborns, her mate does the hunting for the family and brings home the bacon in the usual wolf fashion: He gorges himself with as much as he can hold and regurgitates it in the den. As the pups begin to reach the weaning stage, both parents occasionally leave the den to go hunting.

Like most predators, young coyotes begin practicing their hunting skills at an early age. It's a comical sight to see the awkward pups, seemingly all ears and feet, learning to stalk and pounce on such formidable prey as beetles, grasshoppers, or even rolling tumbleweeds. I once watched a young coyote spend over an hour trying to eat a box turtle. Every time the coyote pounced, the turtle withdrew into its shell. The coyote would stand off a ways and wait for the turtle to reappear, after which the performance was repeated. Perhaps the coyote actually believed it would eventually triumph, or maybe it was just playing; in any case, the turtle didn't seem to be enjoying the game.

As mentioned earlier, the range of *Canis latrans* has expanded tremendously in the past century, and possibly the total population has increased as well. This doesn't mean that coyotes have an easy life of it; their world is a dangerous one.

The coyote's worst enemy is, of course, the human race. People kill a lot of coyotes, both deliberately—through guns, traps, and poison—and unintentionally, mostly with automobiles. Many a young coyote, on its own for the first time and seeking out a new home range, fails to make it across the highway.

Even disregarding the hand of mankind, there are lots of other ways for a coyote to cash in its chips. Although many lower life forms are born with an instinctive sense of what's dangerous and what's not, most mammals must acquire such knowledge through their parents or by the heavy hand of experience. Young coyotes who have never learned better could be blinded by a shot of skunk musk in the eyes, or wind up with a mouth full of festering porcupine quills, or die of rattlesnake bite. Rabies, distemper, and plague take their toll. Sarcoptic mange, carried by mites, can so weaken a coyote that it is unable to survive the winter. In areas where larger predators exist, they also present a danger. Timber wolves, bears, and cougars have all been known to make a meal of a coyote on occasion.

Despite both natural and unnatural hazards, however, the coyote will no doubt continue to survive. I, for one, feel that the world would be a poorer place without coyotes in it. At times, they have caused me some grief—killing my chickens, destroying my watermelon patch, eating the tails off of calves in my charge—but I can live with it.

The American West just wouldn't be the same without the yipping and howling of coyotes. I enjoy their "singing" tremendously; so much, in fact, that while I was in the navy I kept a cassette tape of howling coyotes to listen to in my off time. My days were spent in the sweltering machinery rooms of a submarine, listening to the roar of engines and the hammering of air compressors. At bedtime, however, I could put on my headphones and be lulled to sleep by the coyote's howl and dream of where the stars at night are big and bright, deep in the heart of Texas.

CHAPTER SEVEN

Scorpions and Such

Scorpions are remarkable creatures. As a group they're incredibly ancient. They've been going about their simple little lives, virtually unchanged, for countless millions of years. Many scientists believe that life originated in the sea, and that when the first creature to attempt colonizing the land took its first tentative steps up onto the beach, it was probably a scorpion.

Many bygone civilizations regarded scorpions as somewhat mystical beasts, either for good or for evil. A cult of the ancient Egyptians worshipped the scorpion as the physical manifestation of their god, and scorpion motifs are frequently found among the religious artifacts of pre-Columbian America. And, of course, there is a scorpion among the twelve signs of the Greek zodiac, which indicates it was regarded as somewhat important (along with bulls, crabs, twins, virgins, and the other astrological signs. All these things must have been considered important in some way).

Scorpions are not insects, as much of the general public seems to believe. All insects have three body segments and six legs; scorpions have two body segments and eight legs, in addition to a pair of lobster-like claws. The scorpion's abdomen—its rear segment—is further subdivided into twelve more distinct sections. The last five form the telson (tail), and at the end of this is the scorpion's business equipment: a bulb-shaped sack of venom and a sharp stinger with which to inject it.

There are over a thousand different species of scorpion, found from the snowy Himalayas to the jungles of the Congo, and most places in between. Size ranges from the nearly foot-long *Heterometrus swannerderdammi* (try saying that three times, real fast) from India to the half-inch *Microbothus pusillus* of the Red Sea region. Only about twenty members of this diverse group are actually dangerous to humans. Of the ninety-odd types of scorpion occurring in the United States, only one is considered potentially fatal (the Arizona bark scorpion, *Centruroides exilicauda*). Of course, this doesn't mean that a scorpion's sting should never be cause for concern, even if it did happen outside the range of any "potentially fatal" species. Some people react much more strongly to animal venoms than others, and just because the poison of a certain scorpion wouldn't kill you doesn't mean it can't kill me, and vice versa.

The one scorpion sting I ever received was from a specimen of the Texas bark scorpion, *Centruroides vittatus*, which has nowhere near the sinister reputation of its Arizona cousin. It did hurt, of course, something like a bee sting, and caused a little redness and swelling of the affected area (my big toe). Had my assailant instead been *C. exilicauda*, I could have looked forward to severe pain and swelling, numbness, and difficulty breathing, quite possibly followed by violent convulsions and frothing at the mouth. After all that, I may even have died. There is an antivenin available for treatment of serious scorpion stings, but all things considered, this still sounds like an experience I'd just as soon avoid. Nowadays I always shake out my boots before I put them on.

The chemical composition of scorpion venom was developed long before human beings made their appearance, of course, and the fact that it may hurt us is pure coincidence. The primary reason scorpions have a poisonous stinger is to capture their prey (although self-defense is a convenient bonus). Without venom, most scorpions would probably starve to death. They're practically blind, totally deaf, and don't seem to have much of a sense of smell. Their main method of finding prey is to accidentally bump into it, and unless they were able to kill it immediately it would most likely escape.

The scorpion's front segment, called the cephalothorax, is covered by a hardened carapace, or "shield." In the types that have eyes, this carapace is where they're located—up to ten of them. The reason for all these eyes is unclear. It's generally believed that they can barely detect the difference between light and dark. However, it's dangerous to try to judge the rest of the world's life forms by our own human experience (which is quite limited, in the overall scale of things). Scorpion eyes may very well perform some other function that is quite useful to the scorpion, although totally incomprehensible to us.

Due to its other sensory handicaps, however, the scorpion has a highly developed sense of touch. The pincers ("pedipalps," in scientific lingo) are covered with various types of sensory hairs called trichobothria. It is theorized that these hairs are calibrated to different levels of sensitivity, so that when the scorpion touches something it instantly knows a great deal about it. Some species have no eyes at all but still manage to find their way around obstacles. Perhaps the hairs are sensitive enough to reveal a blocked passageway before actually touching it. There are also organs in the legs that can detect even very slight ground vibrations.

On the scorpion's underside are yet another pair of sense organs. These are called pectines or sometimes "combs" when in a nontechnical conversation. Presumably, they're for determining the texture of whatever surface the owner happens to be walking across at the time—a handy navigational aid for the sightless. The pectines are noticeably more developed in the male scorpion. It's possible that in addition to being used to feel the ground beneath them, these organs are a sort of chemoreceptor, or primitive smell and taste apparatus, which assists the male scorpion in locating a receptive female. There has to be some way for them to find each other, as they don't generally live in close proximity. In fact, anytime you see two adult scorpions together, the chances are pretty good that either they're having sex or one of them is trying to eat the other one.

When Cupid's arrow does strike, scorpions have a complex mating ritual. Although the details vary from species to species, the basic choreography is for the happy couple to "join hands" and circle around. It may look like a romantic gesture, but it is actually completely practical. If the male were to let go of his bride-to-be before the union was consummated, he might not be able to find her again, and the purpose of the whirling dance is to find a good spot to deposit the sperm capsule. Once again, the male's well-developed pectines come in handy. He leaves his packet of seed on a suitably elevated location—usually a pebble or twig—and leads his mate over it. She then draws the offering into her own genital pore, and a new generation of scorpions is on the way. After this, Romeo tries to make a break for it. But sometimes Juliet catches and eats him before he can get away.

Gestation can take anywhere from a couple of months to a year and a half, depending on the species. The young are born alive and do not pass through any sort of larval stage. They're fully formed scorpions from the instant they make their appearance. The mother forms a "birth basket" with her folded legs to catch the twenty or thirty babies as they're dropped, and they quickly climb onto her back. In the births I've observed, the mother always ate the last two or three of her offspring to emerge. Since all of these births were of captive specimens, I can't be sure if this normally happens in the wild. It could be a natural method of population control or perhaps a way for the mother to regain some of her strength after the delivery. In any case, for a baby scorpion, it doesn't pay to be lagging behind.

The youngsters ride around on their mother's back for a week or so, until the first time they shed their exoskeletons. After this, they're on their own, with no more parental care—or even recognition—of any sort. It generally takes about two years before they reach full adulthood, but this varies among species and also depends on the amount of prey available. Better-fed scorpions mature faster.

Most scorpions fluoresce brightly when exposed to ultraviolet light (the same "black light" so popular for groovy, far-out, room decor back during the Age of Aquarius). Once this phenomenon was discovered, the number of scorpion species described in the scientific texts increased dramatically. Due to their small size, nocturnal habits, and generally low profile, many types of scorpion had simply never been seen (at least not by anybody who was interested). The UV light technique is also utilized by the people who make those souvenir paperweights of scorpions encased in plastic domes. It's the quickest way to locate their raw materials.

Every now and then a scorpion is born with two tails. At one time scientific literature placed double-tailed scorpions in a completely different classification from the single-tailed ones. It's now known that the twice-blessed specimens are merely genetic mutations—"freaks of nature"—and not separate species.

The best-known and most-studied two-tailed scorpion was "Pepe," a female *C. exilicauda* held in captivity at the Sonoran Arthropod Studies Institute. Pepe has since gone on to her reward, but prior to checking out she produced a litter of offspring, all of which had but a single tail.

Observations of Pepe revealed that both of her tails, and their associated stingers and venom bulbs, were fully functional. She seemed to prefer using the one on the right side most of the time but could switch-hit with the left one when necessary. When not in use, the tails were held crossed over each other or arched side by side.

The "And Such" of this chapter's title includes two more unusual arthropods: the vinegaroon (also known as whipscorpion, whiptailed scorpion, grampus, and stingless scorpion) and the solpugid (sun spider, windscorpion, sun scorpion, jerrymander, "Child of the Earth"). Neither of these is venomous, although they look as though they should be.

Various species of the vinegaroon occur in most warm regions of the world. Texas's own *Mastigoproctus giganteus* is one of the largest, up to four inches in length. The "vinegar" in vinegaroon refers to the creature's ability to spray a powerful acetic acid solution from a set of anal glands. Acetic acid, of course, is vinegar, but the type that comes out of a vinegaroon is considerably harsher than the bottled variety in the grocery store. Most kitchen vinegar is about 5 percent acetic acid; vinegaroon juice is closer to 85 percent. This is more than adequate to sting the eyes or cause irritation to the mucus membranes of anything foolish enough to irritate it. The vinegaroon's custom recipe also includes a dash of caprylic acid. This blend facilitates passage of the unpleasant brew through the exoskeleton of other arthropods that may be looking for trouble.

Like its scorpion kinfolk, the vinegaroon is nocturnal. Daylight hours are generally spent under a rock, buried in leaf litter, or some such secluded place. Also like the scorpions, vinegaroons seem to have extremely poor vision and hearing and rely mostly on their well-developed sense of touch. The front pair of legs, immediately behind the pincers, are usually carried extended outwards, to feel the surroundings, much as a blind man might use his cane. It is believed that the whip-like telson ("tail") is also a light-sensitive organ that can let the owner know whether it's dark enough to go on the prowl.

The mating ritual of the vinegaroon seems to be conducted on a much friendlier level than that of the scorpion. Prior to the actual dance, the male strokes and caresses the female with his front legs—sometimes for minutes, sometimes for hours. I've even heard (but not actually witnessed) that this may go on continually for several days. I would assume that the female of the species must be stimulated in this manner for successful fertilization to occur, but I don't know why some should be so much harder to stimulate than others. Hormone levels, perhaps.

Once the diligent suitor has seduced his lady into the proper mood, he deposits his sperm capsule on the ground and leads her over it, much as the scorpion does. Vinegaroons do not give live birth, however. The eggs, when laid, are covered with a sticky mucus-like substance, which adheres them to the mother's belly until they hatch.

The average American nowadays takes a dim view of sharing his or her living quarters with any sort of uninvited "bugs," up to and including the vinegaroon. In some regions, however, the presence of one inside the home is considered good luck. In addition, vinegaroons are efficient predators of many other miniature houseguests, including ants and cockroaches. With this in mind, it would seem to be both convenient and ecologically responsible to keep a vinegaroon or two around. But be careful not to make it angry, unless you plan on getting the ingredients for some very potent salad dressing!

Eremobates pallipes is the most common species of sun spider in the Lone Star State. There are about a hundred other varieties, found in warm, dry regions, but all of them look pretty much alike to a non-expert. Different species can often be distinguished only by dissection and microscopic examination, which is probably a lot more trouble than most of you reading this book would care to go to.

About a third of the entire solpugid is its head, and most of its head is its vicious-looking mouth. This, in turn, is divided into four separate parts: Two are used to catch and hold its prey while the other two chew it into a pulp and shove it down the gullet. This is one of the few creatures in Texas that has never gotten around to biting me, but I've been told that it hurts (and I believe it).

Like the other two stars of this chapter, the sun spider gets around largely by sense of touch. What looks to be the forwardmost pair of legs is actually a set of thick, club-like feelers with which the solpugid probes its surroundings. For such a plump little creature, the sun spider can run amazingly fast, which probably accounts for the "wind" in windscorpion. It's also a quite competent climber, using feelers, legs, and oversized mouth parts to secure a purchase on whatever surface it's scaling.

Unlike most arthropods, the sun spider has a tremendous appetite and spends most of its waking hours looking for something to eat. Insects and other small invertebrates (including its own kind, with no apparent remorse) are the normal food items. Small reptiles and amphibians and even mice may be eaten also. They are liable to be on the prowl both day and night. Although they seem to have been designed for a life in the darkness, I sometimes come across one hunting in the hottest part of the day, under the scorching desert sun, driven by hunger, I suppose.

Adults are about an inch long and yellowish-brown. Both sexes look similar, but the females tend to be a bit longer and chunkier in build than their men folk. The males usually have longer and more slender legs.

As is the norm with critters of this sort, the male deposits his sperm capsule on the ground and guides his mate over it. Once this is completed, the female digs out a nest area in the soil, lays her eggs, and stands guard until they hatch. The youngsters are independent immediately (none of that piggyback stuff like the scorpions practice). As soon as they hatch, they wander off looking for something to eat. And that's pretty much the way the rest of their lives will be spent.

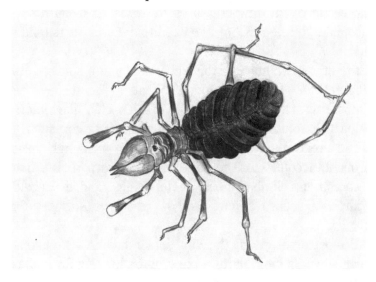

Chapter Eight

Kangaroo Rats

I've spent a lot of time wandering about in the deserts of the Southwest. When I was a little bit younger (and a whole lot stupider), I prided myself on traveling light and "living off the land," including finding my own drinking water along the way. I finally gave up on traveling quite so light after my delirious and nearly dehydrated self had to be rescued by a couple of Border Patrol agents who happened upon my tracks. (This was a fortunate coincidence. I had recently done an economical repair job on the soles of my boots by gluing on pieces of an old tire. The resulting prints looked remarkably similar to those of huaraches, the homemade sandals worn by many an unauthorized border-jumper, so the agents had followed them.) Had they found me a few hours later, they would have been shooing the buzzards off of my lifeless carcass.

Humans, you see, are just not desert animals. A few varieties of us—those races which have had thousands of years of desert life in which to adapt—are slightly better suited to the climate than others, but they are still not true desert animals. When there's no water available, an Indian from the Mojave or a Tuareg from the Sahara will die of thirst just as will a Tahitian or a Swede. We all must drink to survive.

There is another mammal, however, that never drinks. Kangaroo rats often live out their entire lives without so much as a single drop of water crossing their lips. Now that's a true desert animal! Of all the clever ways in which nature has adapted different species to get along where water is scarce, the kangaroo rat's is both the simplest and the most efficient: It simply does without.

Other creatures can get along with little or no drinking water, but most of these cheat a bit by eating succulent foods. The roadrunner, for example, rarely drinks but no doubt receives ample liquid from the plump bodies of the snakes and lizards it devours. The jackrabbit rarely drinks, but it eats a lot of juicy green vegetation. The kangaroo rat not only never drinks, but lives almost entirely on dry seeds. How it can do this is a miracle of biochemistry: It manufactures the water it needs inside its own body.

As most everyone knows, water is a compound of hydrogen and oxygen. Not too many of us have the necessary skills and equipment either to isolate these two common elements from our surroundings or to combine them into water, but the kangaroo rat is born with that ability. Its seed-rich diet, being mostly carbohydrates, is therefore largely hydrocarbon, and the "hydro" in hydrocarbon is, of course, hydrogen. The second ingredient of the recipe, oxygen, is obtained simply by breathing. Inside the deceptively simple looking body of the kangaroo rat, atoms of hydrogen from the food and atoms of oxygen from the air become molecules of water—all the water that's needed. The little rodent goes about its daily business of eating seeds and breathing air, and the water takes care of itself automatically. I've often wished that I could somehow acquire this metabolic function myself so I wouldn't have to lug around so much drinking water on my desert sojourns, but in reality it wouldn't be practical. A five-ounce mouse can find enough available carbohydrates to pull off the process; however, it would take an awful lot of seeds to manufacture enough water for my two-hundred-and-then-some-pound body. Instead of carrying a canteen, I'd just have to haul around a sack of dried corn.

Kangaroo rats are actually neither rats nor kangaroos but form a family of their own. There are twenty different species, of which five are found in Texas. All belong to the genus Dipodomys, which accounts for them being collectively known as "Dipos" in naturalist jargon. Most of them have little to no effect on human activities and have therefore never been the object of any great extermination campaigns. At times various types of dipos have been accused of raiding grain fields or lowering the quality of grazing land by hoarding native grass seeds, but I doubt that this would normally have any serious consequences.

Because their bodies always contain water even when there's none available elsewhere, kangaroo rats are considered prime eating by just about every predator that shares their territory. To coyotes, rattlesnakes, bobcats, foxes, hawks, badgers, owls, ring-tails, and even roadrunners, the sight or smell of a kangaroo rat is like an illuminated billboard saying "Eat Me!" The fact that any species of Dipodomys still exists, when so many other creatures are after it for dinner, speaks well for its speed and agility.

All twenty species look very similar. They also look very similar to a number of distantly related rodents: the jerboas, found in Africa and Asia; and to a small Australian marsupial, also called the "kangaroo rat" (but perhaps should be called the "rat kangaroo" instead). This superficial resemblance is a result of common adaptation to common environments, such as happened with the vultures (see Chapter Two).

As their common title would indicate, the kangaroo rats of America look something like little kangaroos (but are not even remotely akin to them). The hind limbs are well developed, with large flat feet, the forepaws are small and hand-like, and the tails are long. These long tails apparently serve as aids in balancing. Those that have lost their tails through some accident (such as running after the farmer's wife) are noticeably handicapped. Although the tail-less individuals can still leap just as high and as fast as their more fortunate companions, they have a lot of trouble landing. Normally a kangaroo rat alights gracefully on its feet; those without tails hit the ground clumsily and often fall over.

The largest and, in my opinion, most attractive of our five native species is the banner-tailed kangaroo rat (*D. spectabilis*). This is a rodent of the arid regions and in Texas is mostly confined to the Trans-Pecos. It seems to be partial to hard, stony soil and is not known to occur in either cultivated areas or sand dunes. The presence of these little rodents is plainly advertised by the mounds they build—sometimes as large as three feet across. These mounds are often complex labyrinths of exits and entrances, sleeping dens, food storage chambers, and blind alleys to fool predators.

The tail, which is about half again as long as the rest of the animal, has a distinctive white tuft at the end (hence the name). The fur is mostly dark buff, with black facial markings—the "spectacles" of the scientific name.

I made friends with a colony of banner-tailed kangaroo rats by feeding them regularly. On moonlit nights I would leave a little trail of grain from their mound to the trailer I was living in, with a larger pile of grain in front of the door. The plan worked almost immediately. The mice would follow the line of seeds like it was Hansel's and Gretel's trail of bread crumbs. When they reached the pile at the end, they would fly into an orgiastic frenzy of stuffing their cheeks with it, and they never paid the slightest attention to me, although I was sitting a couple of feet away.

Eventually the kangaroo rats learned that the pile of seeds was always going to be there, and I was able to dispense with the trail of single grains. They showed remarkably little fear of me, and a couple of times they even crawled over my feet as though I were a natural part of the landscape.

I didn't want the dipos to become completely dependent on human handouts, however. As the time grew near for me to leave the area, I gradually decreased the amount of grain I left out for them until they no longer expected it to be there. On the last few nights I tied Cholla, my pet coyote hybrid, by the front door during the kangaroo rat's former visiting hours, and this was the last straw. They no longer considered themselves welcome. This was all done with the rodents' best interests in mind, of course. It wouldn't be safe for them to grow too friendly with humans as a whole.

Next in size to the banner-tailed is the Texas kangaroo rat (*D. elator*). This is a rare and secretive animal, considered as a threatened species. Its habitat is a small area of the Rolling Plains in the northern part of the state, and it seems to breed only where there is mesquite. Large areas of mesquite brush are continually being cleared for range improvement and housing developments, which no doubt is having a detrimental effect on the Texas kangaroo rat population.

All dipos are mainly nocturnal in their habits, but this one carries it to extremes. It never willingly leaves its burrow until well past sunset and is back in it well before dawn. Supposedly, *D. elator* even refuses to emerge if the moon is full. This is a true creature of the darkness.

The mounds of the Texas kangaroo rat are much smaller and simpler in design than those of its banner-tailed cousin. They are invariably built at the base of a mesquite, often utilizing the roots as a framework. Although they feed primarily on seeds, as do all kangaroo rats, analysis of the droppings of this species revealed some leaves and shoots in the diet. Whether this was by choice or due to a temporary scarcity of their preferred food is not known.

The Ord's kangaroo rat (*D. ordii*) inhabits most of the western half of the state, from the Gulf Coast up through the Llano Estecado. This is a rodent of sandy soils and is often one of the first animal species to colonize a barren dune. Slightly smaller in size than the preceding two species, Ord's is a handsome little animal with cinnamon-colored pelage and white patches on its face.

As a child I saw a nature documentary in which a kangaroo rat defended itself against a rattlesnake by kicking sand in its face (perhaps the snake later sent away for a Charles Atlas bodybuilding course). At the time I felt that this was probably staged in a confined area. Why would a harmless little rodent stick around to do battle with something trying to eat it, when it could simply run away? Yet, years later, I happened to see almost the exact scene played out between an Ord's kangaroo rat and a bull snake. Although this snake was a nonvenomous variety, it was still more than capable of killing and swallowing the dipo. Yet the feisty little rodent held its ground. As the snake tried to strike at it, the kangaroo rat leaped high in the air, then landed just out of biting range and deliberately kicked sand in the serpent's eyes. I'm not sure how long this had been going on before I showed up to watch, but I saw the action repeated six times. After this, the bull snake must have gotten discouraged, as it turned tail and slithered away. The kangaroo rat made one last kick at its departing enemy, as though to say "And stay away!" If kangaroo rats wore trousers, he certainly would have hitched them up defiantly at that point. Once again, the question arises: Why stay and fight when fleeing the scene seemed so much more logical? All I can think of is that the dipo must have enjoyed the confrontation, but I don't know whether this happens on a regular basis. Perhaps some kangaroo rats are simply more pugnacious than others.

The Gulf Coast kangaroo rat (*D. compactus*) was once considered to be only a subspecies of Ord's. The two look enough alike that I have difficulty telling them apart myself, but I'm taking the word of others (specifically Davis and Schmidt; see the Bibliography) that they are, in fact, two different critters.

The skull of the Gulf Coast type is of shorter proportions than that of Ord's, hence the name "compactus." The tail is also a little shorter and the fur a little coarser. The habits of the two species are similar, with loose sand being the preferred habitat. The primary range of the Gulf Coast kangaroo rat is—you guessed it—the Gulf Coast. It's found on most of the larger islands and on the mainland up to the area of San Antonio.

Last on the roster of the dipos of the Lone Star State is Merriam's kangaroo rat (*D. merriami*). This is one of the true desert species, ranging throughout the Southwest from Trans-Pecos Texas to Baja California. It's also one of the smaller dipos and has a somewhat pale, silky coat.

The Merriam's doesn't seem to be as particular in its choice of habitats as are most other dipos. Perhaps this is due to its broad geographical range, or perhaps the broad geographical range is due to its lack of pickiness in habitat. Either way, the Merriam's kangaroo rat can be found on the type of hard stony soil preferred by the banner-tailed, or in the sand dunes alongside Ord's. This type of adaptability is a useful trait in any species, as it allows for easier survival should the surroundings change.

This kangaroo rat seems to enjoy including a few insects in its diet, along with the usual seeds. I've seen them catch and eat grasshoppers on several occasions, and it wasn't the desperate act of a starving animal. These were plump and well fed, and there were plenty of seeds around. Like other dipos, the Merriam's stores food in its burrow as a hedge against hard times, but I think they eat the grasshoppers simply as infrequent snacks. I've never found anything other than seeds in any of their storage chambers.

One of the characteristics of kangaroo rats in general is that they tend to be quarrelsome with other members of their own species. Two adults confined in close proximity invariably wind up fighting—sometimes playfully, often to the death. Merriam's is apparently a bit kinder and gentler than the rest of the dipos; they don't usually come to blows. This is, in fact, the only variety I know of in which more than one adult can be found living in the same den chamber of a burrow. All the others are confirmed singles.

Taken as a whole, the *Dipodomys* tribe is a fascinating branch of the wildlife of Texas. It's unfortunate that their common name of "rat" carries unpleasant connotations with much of the public. Had the little rodents been called "kangaroo hamsters" or "kangaroo gerbils" instead, people would no doubt look upon them more favorably.

CHAPTER NINE

Hawks

Texas is remarkably rich in its variety of hawks. Many species that your standard textbook or field guide will list as "Mexican" or "Central American" in their range are actually found here in the Lone Star State as well. In addition, we also play host to most of the standard U.S. varieties. Out of twenty-five recognized hawk species native to this continent, twenty-one occur in Texas.

But what, exactly, is a hawk? According to *Van Nostrand's Scientific Encyclopedia*, hawks are "Birds of prey with hooked beaks and large curved claws, closely related to the eagles, falcons, harriers, and others and not sharply distinguished as a group." The last phrase is the clincher: Whatever makes a hawk a hawk is "not sharply distinguished." What are hawks to one person may be "eagles, falcons, harriers, and others" to the next. In my opinion, the birds in this chapter are all hawks. Feel free to disagree.

Many types of hawk have had a rough time of it over the past couple of decades. Besides being wantonly slaughtered as "undesirable predators," the ones that escaped death by shotguns faced an insidious threat from pesticide contamination. The now outlawed chemical DDT, and probably other toxins as well, resulted in several breeding seasons' worth of eggs being abnormally thin-shelled. Most of them broke before hatching. Fortunately, birds of prey in general are making a comeback, but all remain protected by law.

"There's a hawk, Dad." When my son was small he enjoyed spotting wildlife (or anything else, for that matter) before I did, so I usually let him make the first announcement of anything we happened to come across.

"Yeah, I see it now. Can you tell what kind it is?"

"It's one of our hawks!" This was the standard identification and was always followed by childish laughter. Sometimes it was, indeed, a Harris' hawk (one of *ours*), sometimes not. To a five-year-old, it didn't really matter. None of his friends had their own hawk.

In truth, I can't think of a better hawk with which to share my surname. *Parabuteo unicinctus* is one of the handsomer birds of prey around: body plumage a rich chocolate brown with reddish highlights on the shoulders, thighs, and underwings. The finishing touch is a long black tail with a broad white band at the tip—classy, but not flashy.

Good looks aside, the most noteworthy characteristic of the Harris' hawk is that it is frequently found in cooperative groups of up to six or eight adults—extremely unusual behavior. Most species of hawk hunt alone or in pairs at most, but this one organizes itself into efficient commando squads. A team of Harris' hawks will often take up positions surrounding a clump of brush that is likely to shelter rabbits, while one member rushes in to flush out the prey. The rabbit's instinctive reaction is to bolt for another patch of cover, a gambit that usually works against a single predator. In this case, however, the hapless hare is bushwhacked by the other hawks. The successful hunters share the catch among themselves—another oddity among raptors, which usually tend towards selfishness—and move on to do the same thing again. The rabbits almost always fall for it.

The nest of a Harris' hawk is a roughly bowl-shaped platform of sticks, lined with leaves or grass. Most of the nests I've found have been in mesquite trees, but I've also seen them in cottonwoods and in larger stands of cactus. Two or three eggs seems to be the standard clutch size. Although one brood a year is the norm, periods of good weather and abundant food supplies will sometimes result in a second, or even a third, group of youngsters being produced.

Further evidence of the Harris' hawk's cooperative personality comes with the raising of the young birds. Unmated adults sometimes designate themselves to be "godparents" to a breeding pair's offspring and assist in the upbringing. Field studies have shown that nestlings raised in such a situation are larger and stronger than those raised by the parents alone—the result of larger and more frequent feedings. Whether these nestlings also grow up to be spoiled brats has not yet been determined. Maybe more studies are called for.

The zone-tailed hawk (*Buteo albonotatus*) is a pretty rare bird in the United States. Here in Texas, it usually sticks to the dry country of the Trans-Pecos and isn't particularly common even in that limited range. I've often wondered why the species isn't more numerous, as it seems to have hit upon a very clever method of sneaking up on its prey—it pretends to be a vulture.

Now, I can't say I believe that the zone-tailed hawk's remote ancestors figured this out on their own and deliberately tried to disguise themselves, but nonetheless it happened. This hawk bears a striking resemblance to the turkey vulture (*Cathartes aura*), and it takes full advantage of the situation, joining flocks of the buzzards as they soar over the desert looking for carrion. Small animals such as mice and lizards instinctively know that vultures aren't generally interested in anything that still has a pulse, so they make no attempt to head for cover until it's too late. One of the "buzzards" turns out to be a hawk, and the unsuspecting victim turns out to be dinner. Surprise, surprise.

The zone-tailed's nest, like those of most other hawks, is a rickety-looking pile of sticks built high in a tree. When there are eggs or young birds in the nest, the zone-tailed hawk defends the territory aggressively. The one nest I've ever come across was high in a cottonwood near Boquillas Crossing in the Big Bend. I watched (from a safe distance) the parent birds bringing food to the two nestlings and found that they seemed to eat an awful lot of frogs. Whether this was because they liked frogs or simply because frogs happened to be plentiful, I can't say.

As mentioned earlier, the zone-tailed hawk is relatively uncommon. Its preferred habitat is a wooded area, near a river, in a desert—not the easiest accommodations to locate, even in Texas. The only specimens I've ever come across in the wild were the nesting couple I mentioned earlier. Of course, I might have seen others, but I probably thought they were turkey vultures.

Another raptor that just barely ranges into the U.S. is the white-tailed hawk (*Buteo albicaudatus*). This is basically a tropical species although fairly common in the area of the South Texas Plains. White-tailed hawks are birds of the open country. Their hunting style involves soaring high over the plains, making rapid dives for any unlucky rabbits, quail, or other edible prey that is spotted.

This is an attractive species. The feathers on the head and neck are gray, on the back and shoulders, chestnut; the tail and belly are white with fine gray barring. Immature birds are mostly gray all over with a white spot in the middle of the chest. The tail feathers of the white-tailed hawk are shorter than in many other species, and when perched the bird's wingtips extend past the tail.

The nest is generally built in a fairly low bush or tree, and sites on the top of a hill seem to be preferred. It's a typical hawk-type nest, in other words a bulky and untidy heap of sticks. White-tailed hawks often develop the habit of "adding on" to their existing nest every year, piling on more sticks. On one occasion I know of, the overzealous birds built a nest so heavy that it broke the branch it was built on, and they had to start over in another tree. Whichever member of the pair added that last stick probably never heard the end of it. I'll bet the other one is still nagging about it to this day.

The first Anglo settlers in Texas were probably familiar with the goshawk (*Accipiter gentilis*) of the eastern forests. When they encountered a smaller but quite similar-looking bird of prey in their new homeland, they christened it the Mexican goshawk. Although this title is still used occasionally, the more commonly accepted name for *Buteo nitidus* is simply the gray hawk. The plumage is mostly gray (Duh!) with distinctive barring on the chest and belly and a black and white banded tail.

Coincidentally enough, the gray hawk also flies like a gos-hawk. Most other hawks of the Buteo family hunt by soaring at relatively high altitudes, then swiftly diving down on their prey. Gray hawks fly low over the ground, beating their wings rapidly, or else they wait on a perch until a suitable victim is spotted. This is the common *modus operandi* of Accipiter type hawks (which includes the goshawk, naturally).

The gray hawk is fairly uncommon in Texas, occurring only in the lower Rio Grande Valley and not in particularly large numbers even there. Its nest is a small, dainty affair compared to that of most other hawks and is often lined with leaves. Preferred nesting sites are tall trees along the side of a stream or river.

The male of this species is capable of raising his young as a single parent should the need arise. Most other raptor fathers, it seems, do not understand how to feed their own babies. The nestlings need to have their meat torn into pieces small enough for them to swallow, and male gray hawks will prepare the food in this manner should some misfortune befall his mate. Other male hawks can't quite grasp this concept and will bring back whole animals to the nest, which the young, of course, cannot eat.

The word "falcon" usually makes people think of the pere-grine—that sleek, streamlined, steel-gray fighter jet with feathers, swooping down out of the skies to sink its talons into its prey. "Falcon" conjures up images of bold knights riding forth with hooded birds of prey perched upon their gauntleted fists. "Falcon" brings to mind romance and adventure; "falcon" signi-fies mastery of the open skies; "falcon" means all that is noble and powerful.

Well, fine and dandy. But zoologically speaking, there are a lot more falcons in the world than just the peregrine, and the one which least fits the popular conception of falconhood is the caracara. This is a long-necked, long-legged bird with a Mohawk crest on its head and a patch of bare pink or red skin covering most of its face. Although caracaras do hunt and kill prey, they often seem to prefer feeding on maggots and carrion. A caracara or two will frequently take up with a flock of vultures in hopes of sharing in the pickings should a large carcass be located.

The caracara—also known as the common caracara, Audobon's caracara, Mexican eagle, Mexican buzzard, King of the Vultures, and comancho—is now scientifically classified as *Polyborus cheriway* but was formerly known as *Caracara cheriway*. It ranges from the lower Rio Grande Valley along the coast to East Texas and occasionally strays as far north as the Panhandle. Caracaras are frequently seen perched on a fence post or tree stump near a highway, keeping a sharp eye out for road kill. When nothing dead is available, they go after dinner on the hoof, and they aren't particular about the menu—snakes, lizards, rabbits, rats, tortoises, fish, June bugs, prairie dogs, crawdads, baby alligators, grasshoppers, et cetera et cetera.

Although I've never witnessed the event personally, I have it from reliable sources that a pair of caracaras will sometimes attack a golden eagle and force it to drop whatever prey it may be carrying. What I have seen is a caracara harassing a pelican into regurgitating its latest meal, then dining on the not-so-fresh fish with apparent enjoyment. Not what you'd call an especially wholesome method of feeding, perhaps, but it does show ingenuity and resourcefulness.

Human feelings toward the caracara vary tremendously from region to region, perhaps based on the eating habits of the particular birds in each locality. In some areas the caracara is branded as a villainous predator of poultry, lambs, baby goats, even puppies and kittens (the last two cases are purely hearsay, but quite within the realms of possibility). Elsewhere, caracaras are praised for keeping the rodent population in check and the carrion cleaned up. Both representations are no doubt based on truth; it's all in the way you look at it. Unfortunately, the caracara, like other wildlife, is rarely able to modify its lifestyle to please the human race.

More along traditional falcon lines is the aplomado falcon (*Falco femoralis*). Like the peregrine, this is a sleek, streamlined, noble-looking bird. But unlike the peregrine, it's a bit on the flashy side: a white chest, reddish thighs and belly, and very dark gray—almost black—on the wings and back coming around to form a sort of cummerbund pattern. The initial impression is that this falcon is somehow "dashing." If the peregrine is a sort of avian Sir Lancelot, then this is the bird world's equivalent of the Cisco Kid.

The aplomado (Spanish for "dark gray," by the way) falcon was once fairly common throughout the Southwest but is now officially endangered (no doubt due to misguided slaughter and/or widespread pesticide use, as mentioned at the start of this chapter). Until a recent restoration project was begun in 1985, there were no records of this species breeding in Texas since the 1940s.

Under a project of The Peregrine Foundation, ten nestling falcons were collected in Mexico and raised in captivity for the purpose of reintroduction. The initial releases were not exactly a resounding success. As is the problem with many captive-bred animals, the newly released falcons were unfamiliar with basic survival strategies and were soon killed by great horned owls. Subsequent releases seem to have met with better luck, however. In 1992 a pair was found to be nesting near Brownsville in the lower Rio Grande Valley. A single specimen sighted in the Big Bend region, also in 1992, is believed to have been a vagrant from the Mexican population. More of the falcons have since been released in Texas, and it is hoped that this attractive raptor will once again become a frequent sight in the skies of the Lone Star State.

CHAPTER TEN

The Pronghorn

In most American Indian languages, the word or phrase designating the pronghorn is some variety of "deer"—"small deer," "pale deer," and so on. To most speakers of American English, the pronghorn is an "antelope." Neither of these common terminologies is actually correct. *Antilocapra americana* is neither deer nor antelope; nor is it sheep, goat, ox, ibex, or chamois. The zoologists of the past have always tried to stick the pronghorn in with something else, as though they felt it a crime against nature for any large and conspicuous mammal to stand on its own with no living relations. Eventually, most of these classifiers were forced to admit that the pronghorn is an evolutionary orphan and leave it in a family all its own (*Antilocapridae*, the "goat-antelopes"). Some biologists still insist that this is more properly a subfamily of *Bovidae* (see Appendix A), but at the present time these are in the minority.

In general conversation among people who talk about such things, the term "antelope" is still commonly used. I don't see any real problem with that. After all, "...where the deer and the antilocapridae play..." just doesn't sound right. Whether known in the common vernacular as pronghorn, prongbuck, pronghorned antelope, or just antelope, this is a uniquely American creature with a distinguished lineage. Pronghorns had already been grazing the prairies of the West for a long, long time when the ancestors of the first bison arrived there from Asia. (Speaking of these, "Oh, give me a home where the bison roam" doesn't quite cut it either. Calling them "buffalo" is perfectly acceptable among friends.)

Over the past ten million or so years, various models of the basic pronghorn design were tested and discontinued. Some were bigger than today's type and some much smaller. Some had horns similar to those of the modern species. Others had spirally twisted horns, some had two pairs of horns, some had no horns at all. One species even had an extra horn, complete with prongs, growing on its nose. All of these are long gone now; only the one survives. For some reason, now shrouded in the mists of antiquity, it must have been the best one of the bunch.

As was the case with many a Western creature, the pronghorn first became known to science as a result of the Lewis and Clark Expedition. Not that they were completely "undiscovered" before then. As far back as 1540, Francisco Coronado mentioned seeing herds of "fleet stags patched with white" in what is now Kansas. There's little doubt that those were pronghorns.

Although unique in many ways, the pronghorn's most distinguishing feature is, what else—its horns. These are actual horns, by the way, just as one would find on a steer or buffalo. They're not antlers, like deer have, nor hardened bundles of compressed hairs like the so-called "horns" of rhinos. The basic material of which they're constructed is cornified epithelial cells—in other words, horn.

It's not unheard of for a horned animal to shed its horns on occasion. This has even been known to happen with domestic cattle. However, the pronghorn is the only species that accomplishes this on a regular basis. The black outer sheaths are generally shed in October or November, but the bare-bone core of the horn is not usually exposed. The new sheath begins to grow under the old one in late August or early September, and the one is not dropped until the other is fairly well developed. Apparently this doesn't cause the animals any itching or other discomfort, as they seem to pay no attention to the process whatsoever. I've never once seen a pronghorn make any effort to rub off the old sheath or otherwise hasten its departure. When it's ready to fall, it does, and so be it. Cast-off sheaths are gnawed by rabbits and rodents and, if sufficiently softened by rainfall, may be eaten by coyotes or other scavenging carnivores. My pet Cholla (review Chapter Six if you don't remember her) considered these shed horns to be excellent chew toys and was always extremely happy whenever she happened to find one. Of course, pronghorns are never "in velvet" as are antlered animals (see Chapter Eighteen for more on this). Both bucks and does have horns, but as a general rule the female's are tiny, spike-like things. Even those of the buck are comparatively small; twelve inches is a respectable trophy and sixteen inches an outstanding one. The largest set of horns on which I've ever found reliable data hold the record at twenty and one-sixteenth inches, measured along the curve. (The original owner of these magnificent appendages was taken in Arizona, in 1899.) The normal shape of the horns is similar to a thick-handled barbecue fork with one tine broken off and the other one bent backwards. (What? Your backyard barbecues don't ever get that rowdy?) "Freak" horns of various shapes and sizes aren't terribly uncommon. I've seen them with one of the prongs reduced in size or even missing entirely. Sometimes one or both will curve in, or forward, instead of back. I've even heard—not seen with my own eyes, mind you—of a pronghorn buck with three prongs on each horn instead of the customary two. "Old Pitchfork" was supposedly a sought-after trophy for many years but always managed to vanish into thin air whenever the season opened. I've never been able to find any hard evidence that he actually existed or discover what finally happened to him assuming he did exist, but that's all right. Legendary animals, like legendary people, tend to lose a lot of the magic if you ever actually meet one in the flesh.

After the unusual headgear, the most noticeable thing about pronghorns is the rump patches. Each cheek on the south end of a northbound pronghorn is clad in a distinctive patch of white hair. By a remarkable system of muscular control, the animals can "flare" these patches—erect the hairs on them. When a pronghorn does this, the rump patches, fairly conspicuous to begin with, stand out in the bright sun like lighthouse beacons on a dark and foggy night. It seems to be frequently used as an alarm signal to other pronghorns in the area, and it always catches their attention immediately.

Regional folklore—whether Indian in origin or more recent, I don't know for certain—once held that pronghorns can send elaborate messages to each other through alternate flaring and relaxation of these patches. I can remember one of my goals as a very young child being to learn this language. I imagined that there was some mysterious Morse code-like cryptology involved. (I had no rump patches of my own, of course, but figured I could rig up some mechanical substitution that would suffice.) Alas, my dreams of holding intensive semaphore conversations with the pronghorns never materialized. To the best of my knowledge, a flared rump patch has only one meaning: a warning of possible danger in the vicinity.

Pronghorn flesh has always been one of the staples in the diet of the Plains Nations. Although not as valuable, overall, as buffalo—considerably less meat per package and with a hide too thin to be particularly useful—pronghorns were still an important part of the life of most tribes that shared the range with them. In addition to being a source of protein, the pronghorn was a significant medicine beast. Perhaps due to its ability to shed its horns, it was widely believed that various parts of the animal could help the ailing to "shed" their illness.

Prior to the invention of motor vehicles, the pronghorn was the fastest thing in the Western Hemisphere. Many predators—grizzlies, wolves, coyotes, cougars, and bobcats, to name a few—were more than willing to feed on pronghorns. However, except in very unusual circumstances, the only ones they ever tasted were very young, very old, or incapacitated in some way. Catching a prime specimen was simply beyond the capabilities of most other creatures. In fact, today's pronghorns are much, much faster than they really need to be in order to escape from their natural predators. Fossils may shed some light on the reason for this apparent overcompensation. Until quite recently (from a geological perspective), the North American prairies were also inhabited by cheetahs. As most people are probably aware, outrunning a hungry cheetah is no easy trick, but the pronghorn evolved with that task in mind.

Sneaking up on a pronghorn is next to impossible. The animal's eyesight is remarkably sharp. It's often written that a pronghorn's normal vision is equivalent to that of a man looking through eight-power binoculars, although I'm not sure how anybody could know this. (Did they get a test herd of pronghorns to read an optometrist's chart from across the prairie?) As a general rule, though, if you see a pronghorn, it saw you a long time ago.

Although blessed with super vision and able to run faster than a speeding bullet, the pronghorn is a miserable failure when it comes to leaping tall buildings at a single bound. They don't like to jump over anything; in fact they seem actually to be incapable of it. Tests have shown that some individuals eventually overcome this psychological block, but most pronghorns never do. When it comes to a fence, the pronghorn will follow along its length until it reaches an opening or, depending on the type of fence, it may attempt crawling under it. But it simply won't jump over it. A seven-foot fence won't even slow up a white-tailed deer, but a four-foot fence can effectively keep a herd of pronghorns confined. If a fence is keeping them from reaching food, they are more likely to starve to death than to try to jump over.

Crawling underneath a fence can sometimes be hazardous as well. I once came across a pronghorn doe that had become entangled in barbed wire. It looked as though the bottom strand of the fence had snapped and coiled around her, while she was attempting her limbo act. In her subsequent panic, the thrashing had wrapped her up beyond hope of escape. Coyotes or free-roaming dogs had found her in this helpless condition and had apparently just been startled off by my approach. When I reached the doe, I found that one of her forelegs was stripped to the bone, and about half of her face had been eaten off as well. She was still struggling weakly when I did the only thing I could for her—put a forty-five-caliber slug in her brain. I hauled the pitiful carcass away from the fence I had come to repair, knowing that the local scavengers would soon make use of what was left of it. Later that afternoon I noticed buzzards circling over the spot. News travels fast on the prairie.

They make rifles nowadays that are accurate and powerful enough to bring down something in the next time zone, but men have been hunting pronghorns long before these were invented. Back in the days of bows and muzzleloaders, the easiest way to get a pronghorn within range was by appealing to its curiosity. Most of the modern trophy bucks have learned to suppress this instinct (that's how they lived long enough to become trophy bucks), but not too long ago it would work more often than not. Pronghorns seemed compelled to investigate anything out of the ordinary: something like a pile of brush conspicuously out in the open, or a white cloth flapping in the breeze. Any such thing would lure in a pronghorn for a closer look, and if the hunter was lucky, it would be the last thing the pronghorn ever saw.

Even some present-day individuals will fall for this. One summer morning I awoke from a restful night's slumber in the open air to find a couple of yearling pronghorns standing practically on top of me, apparently mesmerized by the sight. (I know I look a little funny when I first wake up—don't you?—but I think this is the only time I ever drew a crowd.) I'm sure the pair must have seen humans before, or at least smelled them, but apparently I was the first one they had encountered in a prone position. At any rate, they seemed to find me quite fascinating, so we just stared at each other for a while. Eventually I had to get up to answer the call of nature, and my movement seemed to break the hypnotic spell. The pronghorns whirled away and retreated a couple of hundred yards, then stopped to stare at me again. This is another common habit of the species—they always want to get that one last look—and had I been hunting at the time, it would have proved their undoing.

The pronghorn is a sociable sort and usually prefers to live in groups. Herds of several thousand were seen a century ago, but in today's world this is unusual. Twenty to thirty individuals per herd is the maximum in most cases. The time of year determines the composition of the herds. Pronghorns band together in different ways depending on the season. Spring herds are generally segregated by sex: Does, many of them pregnant and soon to deliver, form small groups of their own, while the bucks congregate into gangs of rowdy bachelors. The fawns are dropped during the spring season, with the time varying by climate. Here in Texas, pronghorns may give birth as early as February, although early April is more the norm. Farther north, where spring blizzards are a possibility, fawns are sometimes born as late as July.

As summer rolls around, most of the does have completed their maternity leave, the new crop of fawns are running alongside on their spindly legs, and the herds become co-ed. During this season it's normal to see pronghorns of both genders and various ages together. In areas of sparse vegetation, large groups often gather at waterholes, where there's plenty of succulent plants to eat; however, the pronghorn rarely drinks. Smaller herds are more efficient in these cases, as it prevents any one area from being overgrazed.

With autumn comes mating season—the rut—and the social ambience of the herds changes dramatically. Each mature buck now tries to gather himself a harem, and the younger males are driven off from the group. Eventually, most of these cast-out adolescents regroup themselves into "loser's clubs" of five to fifteen individuals. While their fathers and big brothers are out amassing females, the younger ones spend their time together in mock combat and simulated sex acts. This seems to be an important coming-of-age period in the pronghorn's life.

The older bucks, meanwhile, sometimes fight for real. I've come across documentation of male pronghorns actually being killed in these mating season battles, but I doubt this happens very frequently. The does' reactions to all this sudden attention varies among individuals. Certain females seem to be, for lack of a better term, "in love" with a particular buck. When this happens, even should said buck be driven off by a stronger rival, his faithful mate will stand by her man and run off into exile with him.

This is the exception, of course. The average pronghorn doe will show little or no interest in the dominance duels of her lord and master. If he wins, fine; if another takes his place, well, that's fine too. This sounds a bit callous when judged by human standards but makes perfect sense biologically; it's how the best genes get passed along to future generations.

Every now and then an overzealous buck finds that he's gathered together a bigger harem than he can control. Although his does are with him because he somehow proved himself to be a studly individual (or was the only buck around at the time), they didn't sign any long-term contracts with him. If his attentions seem to be spread too thin, some of his does may wander off in search of something better. Occasionally, while the harem buck is running off one interloper, another will sneak in the back way and make off with some of the does.

The arrival of winter brings an end to the rivalries, and all the pronghorns are friends again. The fires of lust have been quenched in the bucks, and any doe that isn't already pregnant will have to wait until next fall for another try at it. The scattered population of an area—dominant bucks with their harems, unsuccessful bucks who couldn't get a harem, the occasional monogamous couple and the bands of youthful bachelors—amalgamate together into the large winter herds. These herds will be a little smaller by the time the weather turns warm again. The old and the sick and the just unlucky will have starved to death or been taken by predators. With spring, the cycle starts again.

When the first European foot left its print on the prairies of the American West, pronghorns, like buffalo, numbered in the millions. Unfortunately, the population of both of these animals began to decline very rapidly soon thereafter. By the early 1900s it was obvious that the pronghorn was in trouble, and in 1914 the species came under the protection of law (difficult, if not impossible, to enforce in many areas, but it was a start). Numbers increased sufficiently to allow limited hunting in 1927, and the pronghorn has been a legal game animal in most years since then. Hunting had originally been part of the cause of the pronghorn's near demise (market hunters slaughtered them by the thousands to supply the butcher shops of newly established western cities), but stopping the killing didn't stop the decline in numbers. As is the case with many another beast of the wide-open spaces, the pronghorn's biggest problem was loss of habitat. Settlement, agriculture, and the fences that accompany these processes brought about a serious change in the prairie environment. With the current state of the country, it is simply impossible for herds of three thousand or more pronghorn to roam around at will. There just isn't room for such things to happen. Short of the total collapse of civilization as we know it, there will never again be as many pronghorns as there used to be. On the other hand, with sound conservation practices and intelligent wildlife management, there will probably always be some pronghorns around. I'm glad about that.

CHAPTER ELEVEN

The Tarantula

There was a fairly popular song from the seventies with a chorus that went "I don't like spiders and snakes." I think the only reason this song was fairly popular was because so many listeners could identify with that feeling; spiders and snakes have never been overly popular with the American public. Nowadays, both of these creatures are becoming popular as pets, and even the non-fanciers of such things are beginning to regard them with a little less revulsion. But there's still plenty of revulsion to go around. Chapter Nineteen will delve into this subject again, when we talk about snakes; for now the spiders have center stage.

Arachnophobia, the fear of spiders, is a rather common affliction among "civilized" folks, which is really a shame. Spiders are some of the most amazing animals in nature, yet far too many members of the human race are unable to appreciate this, because they're too busy being scared—usually for no good reason. It's true that a few (very few) spiders can deliver a painful, sometimes even fatal bite, but that's not really the point. A great many people, it seems, would as soon take a beating as touch a spider, even when they know perfectly well that it's a harmless variety. It's not fear of being bitten, it's simply fear of spiders. Even those who deny experiencing "fear" of spiders often admit to some other sort of unfriendly feelings towards them: disgust, repulsion, perhaps that time-honored emotion known simply as The Creeps. Few of us are completely free of such psychological baggage, including myself. I honestly like spiders, but that doesn't mean I don't get startled when I suddenly encounter one unexpectedly. Especially a big hairy one.

In recent years it's become quite fashionable to keep spiders as "pets"—a practice once restricted to serious naturalists and weird Addams Family type children. This current popularity is basically a good thing, as it fosters better public awareness of, and appreciation for, spiders in general. The bad part is that the demand for certain species in the pet trade has reduced their wild populations to alarming lows. Some types of tarantula are officially endangered as a result of this but fortunately are now being bred in captivity.

I once heard it said that there was little to go on when choosing, as a pet, between a large tarantula and a small kitten. They're about the same size, they're both furry and soft, and both of them are capable of biting their owner but probably won't. The only real deciding factor is how many legs one prefers his pet to have.

The term "tarantula" commonly refers to the spiders known scientifically as *mygalomorphs*. Not all members of this group meet the description that the word tarantula generally brings to mind: large size (by spider standards), dangerous-looking fangs, and hairiness. But enough of them do that the term has stuck. The original tarantula, however, was something else entirely.

The ancient Roman Empire wasn't always a nice place to be, especially if you were a member of the Plebian class—the non-aristocratic, non-politically connected, non-wealthy type of folks (you know, like most of us). Work was hard, taxes were high, and if any member of the ruling class happened to feel like it, he could have you fed to the lions. About the only happy events in the life of a typical Roman peasant were the Pagan festivals, particularly those in honor of Bacchus, the God of Wine. During these revels, such topics as work, taxes, and the threat of becoming lion fodder were temporarily forgotten in a frenzy of drinking, dancing, and casual sex.

When the Roman Empire decided to embrace Christianity, Bacchus and his kind quickly fell from favor with the upper crust. Pagan festivals of all sorts were outlawed, but hard work, high taxes, and corporal punishment weren't. The Plebians didn't really look at this as an improvement on their situation.

Coincidentally enough, along about this time, certain vineyard workers began to suffer strange side effects as a result of the bite of a common spider of the area. Those "unlucky" enough to be bitten (sometimes whole crowds simultaneously, it seems) were afflicted with severe pain and convulsions. The only way to cure these symptoms, as well as avoid an untimely death, was to consume large quantities of wine and engage in spirited dancing. During the course of this treatment, the patients often became so delirious that they lost control of their moral inhibitions. Both men and women, it seemed, could be brought to a state of unseemly physical arousal (a standard witticism of the time was "Did a spider bite you, or are you just glad to see me?") and would sometimes engage in equally unseemly actions with one another. Not that it was their own fault, you understand; the spider made them do it.

The eight-legged villain that brought about this stake through the heart of good clean living was the original tarantula, now classified as *Lycosa tarantula*. The unusual symptoms of its bite first seemed to take effect near the town of Taranto in southern Italy and soon spread throughout the country. Victims were known as *taranti*, and their curative jig came to be called the *tarantella*. It's now an established Italian folk dance, and no spider bites are required for its performance.

Throughout the centuries, many a great scholar has debated the authenticity of tarantism. There were those who swore it was an actual medical emergency, those who claimed it was naught but a contrived excuse to party hearty, and those who believed it varied by situation. One Doctor Thomas Cornelius wrote in 1672 that the *taranti* were "malingerers, wanton young women, and half-wits" and added that he was unable to find a trace of a spider bite on any of the poor sufferers he examined.

L. tarantula is a species of wolf spider, hence it is big and hairy. Due to its rise to fame, all big hairy spiders came to be called "tarantulas" (especially convenient if you wanted to claim that one of them bit you). The first European explorers in the New World, upon coming across the biggest and hairiest spiders of them all, immediately christened them tarantulas (then, perhaps, poured the wine and struck up the dance band).

There are about thirty different varieties of tarantula in North America. Although the lifestyles of all of these are fairly similar, most of this chapter is based on the desert tarantula, *Aphonopelma chalcodes*, found from Texas to California. Naturally, it's big and hairy (although not nearly as big as its tropical cousins, the so-called bird-eating spiders). Desert tarantulas have legs about three to four inches long, a stout, heavy body, and fearsome-looking fangs. These fangs are primarily used to subdue its dinner, not—as seems to be commonly believed—to murder innocent humans for personal amusement. The bite of a desert tarantula is venomous, of course, but not really venomous enough for most people to be overly concerned about. It's on about the same level as a bee sting. These spiders will very rarely bite a person. I've often picked up wild ones I've come across in the desert, and not one of them has ever made any attempt to bite. How then, you may ask, do I know what the bite feels like? Well, once, I accidentally put my elbow on one that I didn't know was there. I'm sure that, to its feeble arachnid mind, the only choices it saw were (1) be crushed to death by a big clumsy mammal; and (2) bite said mammal to get its attention. In the same situation, I suppose I would have bitten somebody myself.

The desert tarantula prefers to live in a burrow in the ground. Should this not be possible—too little soil over the bedrock, or too sandy to dig a permanent hole in—tarantulas may live in rock crevices or brush piles. On one occasion I discovered one of these spiders which had set up housekeeping in an abandoned pack rat's nest. For the most part, though, they live in burrows. Tarantulas don't spin webs, but they do have silk-producing glands like most other spiders, and they use the silk to line the inside of their homes. Besides adding a touch of class to an otherwise drab residence, this also keeps the loose dirt in place.

The normal diet of these spiders consists of insects and other small invertebrates, but a particularly large and/or ambitious one may take larger prey such as lizards and mice. I sometimes wonder if the tarantula I found in the pack rat's nest might have eaten the original occupant to create the vacancy. It's quite possible, although not exactly an everyday occurrence. Of course, the predator can also be the prey; many other dwellers in tarantula country see nothing repugnant about eating spiders. Birds and lizards feed on them when they get the chance, and even larger animals such as badgers and coyotes might eat one should nothing more filling be available at the time.

Since it doesn't spin a web in which to snare its meals, the tarantula has to go out and hunt for something to eat. If it gets lucky, a suitable victim will happen to wander by to be pounced on; otherwise it will have to chase something down. Once caught, the main course will be bitten, which hopefully will kill it without too much of a struggle. Besides hastening the victim's demise, tarantula venom also liquifies its body. Enzymes in the formula break down solid food into a sort of soup, which the spider can then suck up—it's unable to chew. Even this sucking action is somewhat unusual, as the spider seems to draw a vacuum in the area of its mouth parts through contraction of its stomach muscles.

Should some larger predator show an undue interest in the tarantula, it may try to bluff its way out of the situation by rearing up on its haunches menacingly and baring its fangs. This may *look* dangerous, but even if pressed further the spider rarely attempts to bite.

The next line of defense is the use of urticating hairs. Tarantulas don't wear fur just because it's fashionable in their social circles; that pelt can be a weapon. Under a microscope, the stiff hairs on a tarantula's abdomen can be seen to have numerous hooks and barbs. These hairs, which are also coated with a mildly toxic substance, are loosely enough rooted to the body to be easily scraped off by the spider's hind legs. A sudden blast of them in the eyes or snout has an extremely irritating effect on anything that receives such treatment, including people. Although this won't cause any really serious injury, it tends to cause enough of a distraction for the tarantula to make a break for it. A lot of the tarantulas encountered in the wild will have a bare spot on the top of the abdomen. This isn't the arachnid equivalent of male pattern baldness; it means some other creature tried to get too personal. Whenever the tarantula molts—sheds its skin—a new crop of urticating hairs is found underneath. In areas with cool winters, tarantulas sometimes weave themselves a door to their burrows out of silk and leaves, and a few of the urticating hairs may be incorporated into the design—sort of an unwelcome mat.

If physical violence with a large predator is unavoidable, tarantulas have one more trick. The spider tries to get its attacker to grab it by a leg rather than by a more vital area, and then it simply leaves the leg behind while it beats a retreat. From personal observation, I can say that a seven-legged tarantula seems to run every bit as fast as an eight-legged one. The loss is only temporary anyway; any legs that may have been sacrificed for the cause are replaced at the next molt.

Tarantulas are extremely long-lived by spider standards. Females of the species may hang around for a quarter of a century. The men folks, due to their more hazardous lifestyle, rarely make it past the age of ten or twelve.

The main danger in the male tarantula's career has to do with finding a mate. For most of its existence, *A. chalcodes* is pretty much of a loner, keeping to its own burrow unless out hunting for prey. But when the male has lived this way for a decade or so, he suddenly begins to feel strange stirrings deep within himself. So he leaves his cozy abode and strikes out in search of a mate.

The spider undertakes this journey at great risk to life and limb, and although he may have eight limbs to risk, he has but one life. The quest for a mate may be long and arduous or it may be quick and easy, depending on the population density of the area. Supposedly, the lovestruck spider can smell a female of the species once he nears her burrow, but until he *does* near one of these burrows, he pretty much wanders at random.

The outside world is a dangerous place for the roaming male tarantula. In addition to the usual predators that may try to make a meal of him (and he only has so many urticating hairs to go around), he must deal with the human race. Many people, unfortunately, subscribe to the philosophy that the only good tarantula is a dead one. Every spider traveling through an inhabited area must run a cruel gauntlet of boots and sticks and cans of insecticide. If there are roads to cross, the danger increases even more.

Should the randy tarantula survive the perils of the passage and actually locate a female's burrow, his troubles are still far from over. He can't just walk in the front door and pop the question to his beloved. She's a little bit bigger and a whole lot meaner than he is, and she doesn't take kindly to strangers dropping by. He must first attract the lady's attention, from a safe distance, and then convince her that he is neither an enemy nor an entrée. Some females probably take more convincing than do others.

The actual sex act—that which fertilizes the female's eggs and thus ensures a new generation of tarantulas—is a detached and decidedly unromantic process. The male has to spin himself a sheet of silk, deposit a drop of his sperm on it, then absorb the sperm into his breeding palps (sounds simple, but may take over two hours to complete). These palps are two small, specialized "arms" near the front of his body, apparently serving no purpose except this one (which is, granted, an important purpose).

Once it seems safe enough to approach his bride-to-be, the young swain reaches out and gently taps on her body. Her usual first reaction is to rear up into the standard defensive posture described earlier. With continued patting she eventually calms down. Although they have eight eyes (one for each leg, just like us), none of them seem to work all that well, and most tarantula communication is carried out by touch. Maneuvering himself in front of his lady, the gentleman grabs and holds her deadly (to him) fangs with special hooks on his front legs. This is no doubt a precaution for his own safety. Females don't seem to take mating nearly as seriously as do their partners and may decide in the middle of the act that they'd rather eat a male for dinner than be the mother of his children.

Barring any such calamity, the male extends his sperm-laden palps into the proper orifice of the female, sowing the seed for the future of the species. When this has been accomplished, he beats feet away from there. Sometimes the fickle female makes a lunge for him, deciding to eat him after all, but most often she lets him exit unhampered. This is the full extent of the couple's relationship: The male plays no part in brooding the young.

When the sperm induction has been successful and it comes time for egg laying, the female spins herself a clean sheet of silk for the delivery table. Once the hundreds of soft white eggs have been deposited on this, she spins another sheet over them and binds up the edges into a large, pillow-shaped cocoon. This she guards carefully for a couple of months, until her progeny hatch and chew their way out. The spiderlings remain in their mother's burrow for a week or so, then wander off to establish households of their own. Those that live long enough to make their own burrows lead solitary, hermit-like lives until sexual maturity is reached. Then the boys go out a-courtin', while the girls stay home to receive (and sometimes consume) their callers.

Meanwhile, continuing on his merry way, the stud of this story seeks out other females. The courtship scene is repeated as many times as he is lucky enough to both locate and afterwards escape from the objects of his brief affections. Eventually something will probably eat, stomp, or run over him, but if he has managed to impregnate at least one female before this happens, his job is done. Most males never survive the winter following their expectant fatherhood.

In addition to all the other hazards of life on the road, there is one predator that seeks out tarantulas, and only tarantulas, thus increasing the odds against them even more. This is the tarantula hawk—a large, brightly colored, almost metallic-looking wasp.

There are several species of these insects, all belonging to the genus *Hemipepsis* (or *Pepsis*, in some references). The big (up to two inches long) wasps are vegetarians in their adult stage and live mostly on the nectar and pollen of various flowering plants. As a general rule, they aren't particularly aggressive towards humans, but they can give one of us a painful sting should we happen to push one of them too far. The effects of wasp venom vary with the different species of wasp—maybe even among individuals of the same species—and also according to how sensitive the stingee happens to be. As for myself, I've noticed that the sting of a tarantula hawk is, initially, considerably more painful than that of a paper wasp or yellow jacket, but it subsides sooner and doesn't bring about as much swelling of the area. (Yes, at some time in the past I've managed to push all of these insects too far a time or two. Occupational hazard.)

An interesting bit of insect trivia is that only the female has a stinger (an aculeus, in entomological terms) because the stinger is actually a modified egg-laying device (an ovipositor, again in entomological terms). Somewhere in the distant past, certain liberated females began to eject their eggs directly instead of routing them through the tube-like ovipositor. Then they decided to sharpen the tip of the now-useless appendage and equip it with a couple of sacks of poison, which could be squeezed through it. This ploy became so successful and so well known among the rest of God's creatures as something to avoid, that wasps nowadays have considerably fewer enemies than do stingless insects of comparable size. Many harmless insects have even benefited from this reputation through their resemblance to wasps.

All members of the tarantula hawk's family are what's known as "hunting wasps" because they actively seek live prey. Not for themselves—most, like the tarantula hawk, are confirmed herbivores—but for their offspring. The wasp larva need fresh meat

on which to grow, and the dutiful mother supplies this diet in the form of big hairy spiders.

Much of the female tarantula hawk's waking hours are spent searching for victims. She can often be seen (or heard; her buzz is one of the louder insect noises around these parts) flying low and slow over suitable tarantula habitat, her compound eyes peeled for spiders. Some scientists believe that the wasp's sense of smell helps it to locate its victims, but I've got my doubts about that. On several occasions I've fooled them into looking into "dummy" tarantula burrows, which I constructed myself and which bore no trace of spider scent. If odor plays any part at all in the wasp's hunting activities, it must be a small one.

To the wasps' credit, I can say that they weren't hornswoggled by a black rubber tarantula I planted as an experiment. Perhaps movement of the intended victim is necessary to get their attention, or maybe the material of which the ersatz spider was molded had some type of repellant quality to it. Or, maybe they did think it was real but just weren't in a hunting mood at the time. Experiments like this one are only conclusive if the same results are obtained on a number of different occasions, and my studies are still in progress (more about this later).

The wasp's intention is to sting the tarantula; the tarantula seems to know this. During the actual battles I've witnessed, the spider has always tried its hardest to maintain a head-to-head position with its antagonist, as though some instinct has warned it which end of the wasp is the dangerous one. The tarantula hawk cannot be bluffed with menacing postures, and the stinging hair trick has no effect on it. I've read that the wasp doesn't always win; a lucky bite by the tarantula can prove fatal. However, in every such contest I've been fortunate enough to happen upon, the wasp came out on top. I think this must be the normal state of affairs.

As a general rule, the tarantula is not killed by the wasp's venom; it is paralyzed. The victorious insect digs a hole—or sometimes makes use of an existing one—for the interment of its comatose victim. Occasionally it will even use the tarantula's own burrow for this purpose, which always seemed to me to be adding insult to injury. It then lays an egg upon the spider and buries it alive. When the egg hatches, the maggot-like larva finds itself thoughtfully surrounded by fresh, tender, still-living spider meat. This it feeds upon until it reaches the pupa stage, when it spins itself a cocoon amidst the leftover scraps of its involuntary benefactor. Upon reaching maturity, the wasp chews through its wrappings, digs out through the sand, and emerges into the desert sunshine as a full-grown wasp.

Of course, as happens in most aspects of the natural world, things do not always go according to plan. Certain other wasp species make it their business to intrude on this touching domestic scene. Although their own larvae also require fresh meat, these slackers would rather not go to the trouble of stinging their own spiders. Instead, they cheat some other wasp out of it.

These conniving insects are known collectively as cuckoo wasps, due to the similar egg-laying habits of most cuckoos (see Chapter Five). Different species of cuckoo wasps use different methods to achieve the same goal. Some of them sneak up, while the wasp that did the actual hunting is busy digging the hole for its catch, and lay their own egg in the spider's respiratory opening. Others will wait until the rightful owner has finished burying its victim, then uncover it, lay the egg, and cover it up again. In either case, the egg of the parasite has a shorter incubation time than that of the host. The interloper hatches first, then eats both the spider and the egg it was originally intended for.

Each species of hunting wasp is extremely particular about what it feeds its children. For every type of tarantula, there is one type of tarantula hawk that preys upon it exclusively. Other wasps specialize in other spiders, in cicadas, or even in ants. I think the reason my rubber tarantula didn't lure any takers might have been because it didn't look like the right species (it was a generic, largely featureless, dime-store gag spider). If I can get a decoy that looks like an actual *A. chalcodes*, I might get better results.

In contrast to the careful selection of the mother wasp, the larva doesn't seem to care the least little bit about what it eats. In laboratory experiments, wasp eggs were removed from the chosen host and reared on something else—another spider species, an insect, even a suitably sized portion of ground beef—and grew up into fine, healthy adult wasps. However, the females of these lab-raised specimens would still only hunt for the species they were "supposed" to provide for their own offspring. Apparently this instinct is programmed into their genetic code and cannot be changed, which is actually only logical. If every individual hunting wasp was in direct competition with every other hunting wasp, instead of only its own species, not all of them could survive. And although there are probably people who feel that less wasps in the world wouldn't be such a bad thing, the biodiversity of the planet would suffer for it. And nobody can convince me that *that* wouldn't be a bad thing.

CHAPTER TWELVE

Bats

Bats are another group that has gotten a lot of bad press over the centuries, some of it based on actual fact but a lot of it being total nonsense. Perhaps we humans instinctively resent bats because they're the only mammals who can travel in a way that we can't: They can fly. Other mammals can run, walk, swim, crawl, tunnel, float, jump, climb, leap, and bound. So can we, although not nearly as well as some other species. But we can't fly. Thousands of years of petty jealousy against the bats are ingrained into us. From the time we began to fashion representations of angels and demons, the former had the wings of birds and the latter the wings of bats. We tend to associate bats not only with demons, but also with vampires, witches, haunted houses, and scary stuff in general. Remember when Bruce Wayne first decided on the bat as his superhero logo? He chose this symbol because "criminals are a cowardly, superstitious lot" and a Batman would scare them. Would he have managed to strike equivalent fear into the hearts of the wicked had he instead become Possumman or Armadilloman? Not likely.

Fortunately, modern Americans are beginning to get over some of their traditional animosity and learn to appreciate bats. In addition to being fascinating creatures in their own right, many species of bat are efficient destroyers of bothersome insects, important pollinators of plants, and producers of valuable guano. Nowadays guano is primarily used as fertilizer, but it was once an important source of saltpeter (a component of old-fashioned gunpowder). The bat caves of Texas have been mined for this purpose since the days of the Republic.

Texas has more than its share of bats, somewhat in the same way that it has more than its share of birds. Most of the standard U.S. species plus many Mexican varieties are found here. There are about a thousand different species of bats in the world. Forty-four of these are native to North America and thirty-five of them to Texas. Bats form the largest colonies of any mammal (with the exception of humans, of course), and the largest known bat colony in the world is found in Bracken Cave, near San Antonio—over twenty million individuals. Texas can also boast the world's largest urban bat colony, located beneath the Congress Avenue Bridge in Austin. It's consequently no surprise that Bat Conservation International is headquartered in Austin.

Because bats are nocturnal animals that can function in pitch-blackness, it was long believed that they were blind. Although it's now known that most bats have reasonably acute vision, it's also known that they don't really need it. Experiments along this line have been conducted at least since the 1790s, when an Italian scientist named Lazarro Spallanzani covered the eyes of some bats and the ears of others and released them in a dark room. The ones that could hear but not see functioned perfectly. Those that could see but not hear showed a marked tendency to fly into walls.

Exactly how bats were able to hear the location of a wall remained a mystery for many years. Basically, bats in flight emit high-pitched sounds and their paths are guided by the echoes of these sounds bouncing off objects in the way. This method of navigation, technically known as echolocation, is the basic principle behind the electronic device called sonar. Oddly, sonar was not inspired by the echolocation of bats (or dolphins, which also use it). After sonar was invented, a biology student named Donald Griffin realized that bats might be doing the same thing. Experiments proved him right.

Each individual bat, of course, needs to concentrate on its own echoes and not those of the possible millions of its friends and neighbors. Various ways of accomplishing this have been developed, which accounts for many of the unusual facial features of the animals. The heads and faces of bats are amazingly variable. There are bats that look like bulldogs and Chihuahuas, foxes and horses, mice and monkeys and raccoons. Some bats remind us of Halloween jack-o'-lanterns, or the gargoyles on Notre Dame, or the Yoda character from *Star Wars*. And there are many bats whose faces look like nothing else ever imagined. If they didn't have eyes in them, we might not even realize that they *were* faces. All of this is apparently an adaptation to the echolocation system rather than any sort of cosmetic function, which seems to be kind of a relief. I can't imagine having a face like some bats have, without a damned good reason for it. They're lucky they live in the dark and don't have to look at each other.

The best-known bat in Texas is *Tadarida brasiliensis*, commonly called either the Brazilian free-tailed bat or the Mexican free-tailed bat; they're varieties of the same animal. These are the ones that make up most of the huge colonies, Bracken Cave and Congress Avenue included. They are also the predominant bat in New Mexico's Carlsbad Caverns and many other cave systems throughout the Southwest. Should there be no caves available, the bats will roost in mine shafts, hollow trees, or the darker and less-frequented parts of human habitations. This last habit has led to the Mexican free-tail being known as the "house bat" in some localities.

These bats are insect-eaters and feed mostly on the wing. Moths seem to be the most popular item on the menu, but other flying insects—beetles, winged ants, etc.—are also taken. It's estimated that the Mexican free-tailed bat population destroys up to 18,000 tons of insects in Texas every year. Personally, I can barely visualize even one ton of insects, much less 18,000 tons. If even a small percentage of all those bugs that go down the gullet are agricultural pests, it has to be a tremendous help to farmers and gardeners.

Unfortunately, there's a bad side to all these bats: rabies. Many types of bat are known to be carriers of the rabies virus, and the Mexican free-tailed is one of those most frequently tested positive by the Texas Department of Health. Of course, out of the millions of individual bats, only a small percentage are infected, but caution should be exercised, particularly around any bat that seems to be sick or injured. Anyone bitten by a bat should always seek medical attention immediately.

Another common Texas species is the pallid bat, *Antrozorus pallidus*. In the previous century, pallid bats existed in numbers to rival the passenger pigeon. Although still found in respectable quantities throughout the Southwest, today's population is only a fraction of what it once was. This drastic reduction was probably the result of a number of factors: increased use of agricultural pesticides, disturbance of habitat; perhaps simply increased human presence in desert areas. The relatively recent practice of sealing up caves and abandoned mines for safety reasons has no doubt had an effect on this species and other bats as well.

I spent a few months sharing a run-down cabin with a dozen or so pallid bats. I lived in the main room and they occupied the loft. It amazed me how they were able to squeeze in and out through the narrow crack between wall and roof. Until I actually saw them do it I couldn't figure out their access route.

Pallid bats are somewhat unusual in their feeding habits. Most of their diet consists of ground-dwelling prey such as crickets and other non-flying insects. Scorpions and centipedes are also eaten, even though these animals are quite capable of causing injury to the bat. Speed and accuracy in biting are vital to success, somewhat similar to the way a mongoose kills a cobra. It would seem as though these bats locate their prey by sight, although echolocation may play some part in the process also.

Once its dinner has been subdued and captured, the pallid bat usually carries it to a feeding perch. There it eats, hanging head upwards by its thumbs, and forms a pouch with the membrane connecting its legs and tail to catch any pieces of food that it drops. To the best of my knowledge, no other bat feeds in this way.

The Mexican long-tongued bat (*Choeronycterus mexicana*) rarely strays north of the border but has been recorded in Hidalgo County of extreme South Texas. This species is primarily a pollen and nectar feeder but probably eats a few insects now and then to get some protein in its diet. The ears are relatively small, the muzzle is long and pointed, and the tongue—well, the tongue completely justifies this bat's common name. A human with a tongue of the same proportions could lick himself on the back of the neck.

This magnificent tongue enables the bat to drink the nectar from a great variety of night-blooming flowers, and it probably plays an important role in the pollination of some types. Although rumored to occasionally damage fruit crops in Mexico, captive specimens could not be coerced into eating solid fruit. They would eagerly lap up the juice but made no attempt to chew on the pulp.

The Mexican long-tongued bats, like many other bats, roost in caves, mines, and abandoned buildings but do not form large colonies. They're often found alone or in pairs, with the maximum group size seeming to be about a dozen or so.

Mormoops megalophylla is known, in plain English, as either the ghost-faced bat or the leaf-chinned bat. This is another of the mainly tropical species that reaches its northern distribution limits in Texas.

Whoever first christened this creature as "ghost-faced" must have had some mighty peculiar notions as to what a ghost looked like. "Leaf-chinned" is a little closer to the mark, as there are several leaf-shaped projections in that area. Had I discovered the species myself, I probably would have called it something like "the melted head bat." My first impression on seeing one was that it was a wax figure left in the hot sun or perhaps taken from the mold before it was quite hardened. The facial features—nose, lips, and ears—have been variously described as grooved, twisted, ridged, convoluted, wrinkled, crinkled, foliated, saggy, baggy, creased, furrowed, puckered, and rumpled. You get the idea. This is one homely critter!

These bats roost in large groups. A colony of over six thousand was discovered in Frio Cave (Uvalde County), and some caverns in tropical Mexico are estimated to hold over half a million. Unlike many other gregarious bats, however, *Mormoops* seems to need "elbow room"; rather than cling together in clusters, individuals space themselves out evenly. Because of this characteristic, a colony of ghost-faced bats requires a bigger cave than would the same number of most other species.

No discussion of bats would be complete without mentioning that nightmare incarnate, the vampire bat. Based on informal polls I've conducted, it seems that the average American thinks vampire bats are only found in remote jungles far, far away. Movies and adventure fiction often feature vampire bats in such locales as New Guinea, Borneo, and the Congo. Indiana Jones casually remarked on the presence of "giant vampire bats" on his way to the Temple of Doom, which was supposedly in India.

Well, surprise, surprise. Not only are vampire bats unique to the Western Hemisphere, but they are quite common only a few hundred miles south of the border and have been found in Texas! In fact, some experts believe that vampire bats are on a slow but steady northward expansion and will soon invade our country in much the same way as killer bees and fire ants have recently done.

There are three known species of vampire bat, and all three have been known to cross the border into Texas. The common vampire (*Desmodus rotundus*) is believed to be the only one that feeds on human beings. Fortunately, this particular bat seems to have visited Texas in the past, found the area not to its liking, and gone back home to Mexico. Semi-fossilized bones are frequently discovered, but as far as I know the living animal has never been recorded within the Lone Star State. However, the species has been collected in the Mexican state of Nuevo Leon in areas less than a hundred miles from the border. And a hundred miles isn't too great a distance, as the bat flies.

The two lesser known vampires are the hairy-legged (*Diphylla ecaudata*) and the white-winged (*Diaemus youngi*). Both of these are also found in Mexico, not too far from the U.S. border, and are apparently expanding their range. Like its common cousin, the white-winged vampire is only known from bones here in Texas. The hairy-legged, however, has been found here in the flesh.

On May 24, 1967, a man named Remington shot into a cluster of bats in an abandoned railroad tunnel in Val Verde County. One of the "trophies" thus obtained turned out to be a hairy-legged vampire, and a minor panic occurred after the identification was made. I'm sure that most of the population of Val Verde County had never before been fed upon by a vampire bat, and I'm equally sure that most of them wanted to keep it that way. There were also economic considerations. Large numbers of vampire bats feeding on cattle and goats can do serious damage to the livestock industry.

These fears were apparently unjustified. Not only was this the only vampire bat ever documented within almost five hundred miles (to the best of my knowledge, no more have been found to date), it was also the most harmless variety. The hairy-legged vampire seems to prefer the blood of birds over that of mammals and has never been known to attempt feeding on a human. It also occurs in small groups rather than the huge colonies of its better-known relation. All things considered, if you have to have vampire bats around, the hairy-legged species would be your best choice.

CHAPTER THIRTEEN

The Mockingbird

The very word "mockingbird" would imply that this is a creature that frequently imitates others, and the scientific name—*Mimus polyglottos*—can be roughly translated as "the multilingual mimic." Most native terms for the mockingbird also referred to this ability. The Choctaw tribe knew it as hushi balbaha, "the bird which speaks many languages." Mimicry is only one aspect of the mockingbird's complex personality but seems to be the one that caught the fancy of both the zoological community and the public as a whole. Granted, the mockingbird is very talented at—well, "mocking"—the calls of its feathered kinfolk. Individuals of the species have also been known to do passable imitations of other, non-avian, sounds: whining dogs, hissing cats, squealing piglets, rusty gate hinges, even wolf-whistles and car alarms. Why does it do this? Apparently because it enjoys it.

Folklore contains various other explanations. According to one tale, the mockingbird was the feathered favorite of The Creator and was the only one given a voice. The other birds began to grow jealous of this preferential treatment, so the mocking-bird—benevolent soul that he was—agreed to teach them to sing. Some pupils, the ones that became known as songbirds, displayed a better aptitude than others and acquired a fair degree of musical talent. Others—ducks, geese, crows—could only manage a few unpleasant sound effects. Eventually the mockingbird lost interest in tutoring, and all the birds were stuck for eternity at whatever level they had reached at the time.

Mimicry is something of an amusing hobby, but its own song is its true talent. The voice of the mockingbird has been admired for centuries. Thomas Jefferson once wrote an essay in which he patriotically boasted that the American mockingbird's song put that of the European nightingale to shame. And according to Henry Wadsworth Longfellow, the mockingbird makes such beautiful music that "the whole air and the woods and the waves seem silent to listen."

In 1855 the American composer Septimus Wilburn "borrowed" part of the mockingbird's melody and put lyrics to it. He originally saddled this musical creation with the somewhat pompous title of "A Sentimental Ethiopian Ballad," but for over a century it has been popularly known as "Listen to the Mockingbird." Just about everybody in America knows at least part of the lyrics, and snatches of the tune frequently turn up in movie and cartoon soundtracks. It was the theme music for Heckle and Jeckle, despite the fact that they were supposed to be magpies. The Three Stooges also used it as their trademark song before switching over to the more appropriate "Three Blind Mice."

Any bird as popular as this one would naturally make an acceptable showing when it came time to choose official state symbols. *M. polyglottos* has been designated the State Bird of Texas and also that of Arkansas, Florida, Mississippi, and Tennessee.

According to my research, both the men and the women of Texas approved of the mockingbird's selection for this honor, but for different reasons. Our female population, as represented by the Texas Federation of Women's Clubs, first petitioned for the mockingbird in 1927. Their fondness for the creature was based largely on their appreciation of its singing voice. The men folks of the State Legislature added to the resolution that the bird was "a fighter for the protection of his home, falling, if need be, in its defense, like any true Texan." The voice of an angel and a spirited scrapper as well—who could help but admire this creature?

Our particular variety is only one of many mockingbird species. Its usual common name is "Northern mockingbird" due to its natural range. Most of its kinfolk live South of the Border, from Mexico down to Patagonia. Deliberate introduction into

Hawaii has led to a local population there as well, and there are possibly a few descendants of escaped cage birds living in jolly old England.

Defense of the home turf is a fairly common character trait among many species of birds (see Chapter Five for more about this). We often speak of being "free as a bird," but this is misleading. The majority of our feathered friends spend their not-so-carefree lives confined to one small area, and they put in a good share of their time trying to run off interlopers. I once heard this territorial instinct described as "nature's invisible cages"—an accurate metaphor. There may not be any bars or chains in sight, but the birds are virtually imprisoned nonetheless.

The mockingbird is one of the more high-profile defenders. Less aggressive birds may content themselves with scolding an intruder from a distance or trying to lure it away with the old pretending-to-have-a-broken-wing trick. Not so with the mockingbird. He hitches up his trousers, spits on his hands, and dives into the fray. A mockingbird will attack whatever encroaches on its domain, be it eagle or alley cat or unsuspecting postal carrier. If a *T. rex* happened along, the intrepid bird would probably attack that just as readily. One of John J. Audubon's most famous bird paintings depicts a trio of mockingbirds in valiant combat with a rattlesnake.

Different mockingbirds seem to form their own opinions as to the appropriate size of their personal no-entry zones, as shown by the following example. Two large bushes at opposite ends of a San Antonio city park each contained a mockingbird nest. One of them belonged to what must have been a particularly irritable pair. Anyone approaching within about fifteen feet was attacked, sometimes by the male alone but frequently by both. Unfortunately, this restricted area included both a drinking fountain and the most direct path to the tennis courts, so many an innocent passerby suffered the unexpected wrath of the mockingbirds. When one particularly vicious tandem attack drew blood from the scalp of a tennis player, he killed the female bird with his racket—a bit of an over-reaction, perhaps, but somewhat understandable. Someone else later took the orphaned eggs and tried to artificially incubate them, but they never hatched.

Couple Number Two were much less flamboyant in their actions. Although they, too, had a nest in the park, they made little advertisement of the fact. The nest's presence wasn't even suspected until the male swooped at a boy trying to retrieve an errant ball from the foot of the bush. Most people left the mockingbirds alone, and they reciprocated. And after a couple of weeks there were five babies in the nest. A month more and there were five new mockingbirds to fill the air with their music. Sometimes, it seems, it doesn't pay to defend one's neighborhood *too* vigorously.

Mockingbirds seem to mate for life, or at least for a fairly long time. During the winter months each bird leads a solitary existence within its own "invisible cage" and will tolerate no companionship, not even its own mate. When spring rolls around, the couples reunite for another season of raising a family. As a general rule, mom does the incubating while pop protects the area and sings a lot. Despite the general appreciation of his music, some people can begin to feel that he overdoes it. The mockingbird often begins singing at sunrise and never shuts up throughout the day. And if it's a moonlit night, he may keep at it till the wee hours.

The mockingbird's menu varies with the season, but insects are the preferred food. When these are abundant, they make up most of the diet. The mockingbird will sometimes perch on an elevated position, keeping a lookout on the ground below, and swoop like a falcon on any prey it spots. On other occasions it may ground-hunt. The usual routine for this is to take a few steps, slowly open its wings to flash the white patches, take a few more steps, and so on. Nobody seems to be entirely sure what this is all about. I've heard it said that the sudden flash of white scares insects out of their hiding places. At any rate, the method seems to work; mockingbirds rarely have any trouble feeding both themselves and their families with plenty of caterpillars, grasshoppers, and beetles. Insects naturally become scarcer during the winter, and the mockingbird switches its attentions to such available fare as seeds and berries.

Mockingbirds have adjusted well to civilization. Suburban parks and gardens suit them just as well as the undisturbed wilderness used to do. Although there are occasional differences of opinion with the human inhabitants (and their pets), they seem to do all right for the most part. It's been reported that city mockingbirds often stake out smaller territories than country mockingbirds. Perhaps this is due to the food supply. It's probably easier to spot edible insects on a neatly mowed lawn than in a tangle of wild vegetation. And, of course, many people put out birdfeeders or raise ornamental plants with berries.

Trying to determine the "intelligence" of any non-human life form is a difficult business (for that matter, it's often difficult with humans as well). We can get other creatures to navigate their way through mazes or learn to avoid receiving electrical shocks as a consequence of certain actions. We can often train them to carry out menial tasks for us or to perform tricks for our amusement. But do any of these things actually prove that one species is "smarter" than another?

With what little criteria we have to go on, it would seem that the mockingbird is one of our more intelligent native species. There are now strict laws concerning the capture and possession of wild birds, but at one time pet mockingbirds were fairly common. Sometimes these captive specimens would do things that could only be described as acts of logical reasoning.

Case # 1: A pet mockingbird developed a taste for canned dog food. The human of the house fed the family canine in the kitchen, and the bird soon memorized the schedule. At feeding time, the mockingbird would conceal itself in another room and imitate the particular whistle the owner used to call his dog. The faithful pooch felt obliged to answer the summons, of course, and while thus engaged some of his food would be stolen. The dog fell for it every time.

Case # 2: A mockingbird kept in a cage by an open window learned to imitate the songs of the wild birds it saw and heard outside. After a while, it began to recognize individual species and would break out into the song of a bird whenever it saw one fly by. One day, quite by chance, the mockingbird happened to see a picture of a cardinal and responded with the cardinal's call. The owner showed the mockingbird other photographs. If they were of a species it had previously observed, the bird would imitate the call; if not, it remained silent.

Case # 3: A farm boy, accompanied by his pet mockingbird, happened to fall into an abandoned well and was unable to climb back out. The bird flew back to the house and, through constant squawking and badgering at the boy's mother, convinced her to follow it. It led her to the scene of the accident, and the boy was rescued. I haven't been able to find out whether this particular mockingbird was named "Lassie," but it wouldn't really surprise me if this were the case.

These are impressive accounts, even if you allow for a modicum of exaggeration in the telling of them. One more thing is worthy of mention, however. The mockingbird has demonstrated a remarkable ability to adapt itself to changing conditions and to flourish in a world overrun with humans. And that, to me, proves that they're pretty damned smart.

The Javelina

Long, long ago, but not so very far away, a diverse family of pig-like creatures roamed the plains and forests. These prehistoric porkers have since been given scientific titles such as *Platygonus* and *Mylohyus*. Their present-day descendants are known to most people as peccaries; in Texas they are more commonly referred to as javelinas (from the Spanish word for javelin; a reference to the shape and sharpness of their teeth). Our local species is the collared peccary, *Tayassu tajacu*.

The javelina isn't really a pig, although it does somewhat resemble one. The two families are probably related, but their similarities are largely a case of what's known as parallel evolution. The true pigs developed in the Old World, while the peccaries developed in the New World but followed the same general path. Most of the physical differences between the groups are relatively minor: slight variations in tooth and bone structure, for example. The major external characteristic that sets the javelina apart from its hog cousins is the musk gland on the former's back. This has always been one of the most noticed traits of the peccaries, as historical literature will attest. It is noteworthy that few early writers showed much interest in the javelina beyond its suitability for human consumption. This was probably due to its resemblance to that familiar dietary staple, the domestic hog.

> The country has of its own a kind of Hog, which is called Pecary, not much a Virginia Hog. 'Tis black, and has little short Legs, yet is pretty nimble. It has one thing very strange that the Navel is not upon the belly, but the Back: And what is more still, if upon killing a Pecary the Navel be not cut away from the Carcass within 3 or 4 hours after at Farthest, 'twill so taint all the flesh, as not only to render it unfit to be eaten, but make it stink insufferably. (1681)

They have, moreover, upon the back, and above the buttocks, what in this country is called catinga, that is, a gland whence flows a liquor like thick serum, which has a disagreeable smell.... (1783)

Although not so large as the European wild hog, it is just as savage, and it resembles the European wild animal in all respects except its back. The back...is much higher than that of the common wild hog. In the middle of its back is a navel-shaped hole from which is exuded a heavy odor of musk, which spreads throughout the flesh and makes it distasteful. For this reason, almost all the Spaniards have an aversion to it. (1795)

It is said, and I believe it; that their flesh is good, but not so fat as that of the hog; when killed, however; the glandular orifice between the haunches must be removed, since, if this is not done, the flesh acquires a bad odor and taste. (1849)

The wild Mexican pig, or jabelin [sic] is a useful source of meat, though the strong flavor requires judicious seasoning. However, should the musk gland in the center of the back not be removed immediately following the death of the animal, the flesh becomes tainted beyond the cloaking abilities of the most pungent spices. (1890)

The flesh of these wild swine is not in much repute, and unless the back gland is at once cut out a freshly killed specimen will become quickly spoiled as a human food-supply. (1917)

We have been served the flesh of the peccary in Central America and found it to be much like pork, but the musk gland must be removed as soon as the animal is killed, or the flesh will be tainted. (1964)

Over the years I've eaten several javelinas. I never failed to cut out the musk gland as soon as possible, because I "knew" the meat would otherwise be ruined. (Everybody knows that; just look at the preceding testimonials.) Lately, however, I've been hearing that this is nothing more than superstition, that cutting out the musk gland of a javelina is simply a traditional action. It may not have any more effect on reality than does throwing spilled salt over one's shoulder. I haven't yet conducted any experiments along these lines (cutting out the musk gland, that is; not throwing the spilled salt), but it's on my list of things to do.

Another "fact" about the javelina that everyone knows is their supposed ferocity. Much of this is complete hogwash (peccarywash?). Granted, javelinas are quite capable of doing somebody injury. (I know from personal experience that even a half-grown one can bite clean through a cowboy boot!) Their tusks, although they grow downwards (for biting), unlike those of the wild boar, which grow upwards (for goring), are long enough and sharp enough to kill hunting dogs—which happens, but usually in self-defense. Most predators realize that a javelina with its dander up is no easy pickings. I've witnessed coyotes and bobcats routed by an angry band of tusk-popping peccaries.

The widespread rumors of javelina horror are, however, largely misconceptions. A South American species of peccary, the white-lipped (*Tayassu pecari*), is apparently much more aggressive than its Texas cousin and also travels in much larger groups (up to a hundred, I've been told). This is the actual star of all those adventure tales where the lone hunter is bushwhacked by a vicious herd of peccaries and forced to spend the night in a tree. Our own javelina is basically harmless to humans, unless cornered and defending itself. Even a mouse is liable to bite somebody under those circumstances.

I thought I was being attacked by a herd (actually, "sounder" is the correct term) of javelinas on one occasion. I was hiking through a deep arroyo—one of those "part-time riverbeds" gouged out by the seasonal cloudbursts of the Southwestern deserts—looking for fossils and basically minding my own business. I smelled and heard the oncoming javelinas at about the same time.

In retrospect, I figure there were about a dozen of them, including babies; at the time I thought there were more like a thousand. They charged around a bend in the arroyo, their little hooves pounding the gravel and their tusks clicking like castanets. They had apparently put their famous musk glands at full power, because the skunkish odor hit me in the face like a fist.

I had suddenly found myself in one of those adventure stories I mentioned earlier, but this one had an interesting twist on the plot. Not only was I unarmed, but there was nary a tree in the neighborhood. After the initial split-second of frozen panic, I turned and ran (well, what would you have done?).

I've never been a fast runner. As a child I was doomed to be "It" for the duration of every game of tag. Whenever I played baseball in high school I'd be lucky to make it to second base on a hit that should have been a home run. But with a herd of javelinas at my heels, you'd better believe I was *flying* down that arroyo. When I reached a point where the walls weren't quite as steep, I clawed my way halfway up the dirt bank and grabbed a protruding mesquite root, which promptly snapped off in my hand.

I landed on my back, hard enough to knock the wind (what little I had left at that point) out of me. It wasn't an overly long fall, but in the little time it took to hit the ground, I resigned myself to being turned into fajita meat by the javelinas. And it was another few seconds before I realized that they were gone. The noise of their passage was already fading away in the distance (the smell hung around a bit longer). I backtracked to where I had lost my hat. (My rapid take-off had probably left it hanging in midair, the way it happens in cartoons.) There were a couple of hoof prints on the brim, but aside from that it hadn't been touched.

To this day I haven't the slightest notion what it was that they were chasing—or fleeing—but it obviously hadn't been me. Their own noise and aroma had probably masked mine completely, and they hadn't even been aware of my presence. Of course, had one or more of them happened to blunder into me during their mad dash to who-knows-where, I could well have been seriously injured. So I wasn't a *complete* fool to run from them, you see.

All my life I've been hearing that javelinas kill and eat rattlesnakes. This is another of those little nuggets of wisdom that seems to turn up in every book with peccaries in it, so I may as well include it in this one as well. Some writers have gone so far as to describe how the rattlesnake, upon realizing there are javelinas in the area, will immediately try to hide itself. (Sometimes this is stigmatized as a "cowardly" act, although the trembling hunter up the tree, often found in the same book, is never tarred with the same brush.) Should one member of the sounder discover the cowering serpent, a call goes out to the others, which immediately surround their victim in vicious glee. As the desperate snake tries to strike at its antagonists, they rush in and pound it to death beneath their sharp hooves.

Well, maybe. . . . A few years back, I was assisting with the capture and subsequent relocation of some javelinas, which had overpopulated their present area. We had six of the animals held in a portable corral made of wire panels while they awaited shipment to greener pastures. Although irritable when first captured, the javelinas had settled down after a few days and seemed to be none the worse for their temporary confinement. This was an important thing to monitor, as captured wild animals often suffer a sort of traumatic stress reaction, which can be fatal, regardless of how gently the captor tries to handle them.

I had been feeding the javelinas on various forms of succulent native vegetation, harvesting it from different spots so as not to denude any particular area. One morning I found a two-foot rattler at the base of the lechuguilla plant I was digging up for my charges and decided to feed it to them for dessert. I saw nothing cruel or sadistic about this. Wild animals, particularly those that are soon to be returned to the wild, should be fed their natural foods if at all possible. Thinking that the rattlesnake was simply a part of the javelina's normal diet, collecting it along with the lechuguilla was a perfectly logical thing to do.

When I put the snake in their pen, all six javelinas watched it crawl from right under their snouts over to a corner and coil there in repose. Then all six raised their heads and gave me a look that silently, yet quite plainly, inquired as to exactly what kind of an idiot I was. Having thus made their feelings clear, both about rattlesnakes and about people who offer them rattlesnakes, they went back to eating their plants. The serpent remained in the corner, ignored and unmolested, until the next day when I took it out and let it go.

I realize that this one incident doesn't mean javelinas never kill rattlesnakes. My previous experience with horned toads (Chapter Three) had already convinced me that just because I had never seen something didn't make it untrue. Maybe certain individual javelinas have a peculiar fondness for snake meat, or a decided unfondness for live snakes, but I've yet to run across any of these. Feral (and most domesticated) hogs will kill and eat snakes on a regular basis. Perhaps past observers had gotten their pigs confused with their peccaries, or they simply assumed that whatever one does, the other will do as well. In actuality, the javelina is a much pickier eater.

Javelinas are primarily vegetarian. They eat a lot of cactus and agave, also mesquite beans, acorns, and various roots and leaves. They have no qualms about raiding a vegetable garden should one be available and will also eat fallen fruit in orchards. Now and again they may dine on a few insects or quail eggs, and maybe they do eat the occasional rattlesnake.

Prickly pear makes up the bulk of the javelina's diet in many places. Although this cactus-rich menu supplies the animals with water—quite useful in arid climates—it doesn't really supply a whole lot else. The nutritional value of the prickly pear is so low that, if fed on it exclusively, a javelina will literally starve to death with a full belly. Cactus is what is considered a "maintenance food," something to survive on temporarily while searching for better provisions. Besides its lack of nutrients, such a diet can cause a build-up of oxalic acid in the bloodstream, leading to possible kidney failure or other metabolic problems.

The javelina is a social animal, usually found in groups of six to twenty. Writers from the previous century report much larger herds, up to several hundred. Perhaps this was simply error or exaggeration on the part of the observer. Groups of moving animals are difficult to count accurately, and it can often seem as though there are more of them than there actually are (especially if they're chasing you!). It could also be that the javelinas have simply adapted their behavior to suit modern times. Should your most serious danger come in the form of a puma, a bear, or a wolf pack—or even an Indian with a bow—there could be greater security with greater numbers. However, once firearms are introduced into the equation, everything changes; larger concentrations of animals become so many fish in a barrel.

A sounder of javelinas has its dominant animal, usually an old boar, but it's not the "leader" in the same sense as would be found in a pack of wolves. In the javelina community there aren't as many rules, and the discipline is not as rigid. This is a common difference between social predators and social herbivores. Bringing down a moose or elk requires much more precise teamwork than does surrounding a clump of prickly pear.

The standard peccary noises (squeal, snort, and grunt) can be combined in various ways to convey messages among the group. There is an alarm call and a call to share in whatever bounty may have been discovered (commonly heard when a javelina comes across a salt block left out for cattle). There are also distinctive vocalizations which can be roughly translated as "Go away, you bother me," "Where is everybody?" and "Wanna go to my place, Baby? Heh, heh, heh." This last one is primarily used by the dominant boar, who rates first pick among all receptive sows within his herd. Javelinas are basically promiscuous, however. Although individuals may show some degree of loyalty to the group as a whole, they don't seem to form lasting pair bonds.

Physical contact is an important aspect of javelina society. They frequently nuzzle and rub against each other and seem to deliberately transfer musk from the glands on their backs. Although one javelina stinks just about the same as another to the untrained human nose, it's possible that this frequent musk sharing creates a combined odor common to all members of a particular group. With their weak eyesight, this would be a reliable way for javelinas to make a quick identification of their own herd mates.

Prior to 1939 javelinas were classified as vermin, and anybody who took a notion to could slaughter them at will. This was partly due to fear (they were often considered dangerous to humans) and partly to the belief that they competed with domestic livestock. Both of these notions are now known to be false. Javelinas often actually "improve" the range land by eating plants that are of no value to cattle. The current designation of the javelina in Texas, New Mexico, and Arizona is as a game animal, and this is as it should be. Game animals are officially entitled to proper scientific management and controlled harvesting in a sporting manner, and the javelina deserves that respect.

CHAPTER FIFTEEN

The Alligator Gar

Fish are supposedly the evolutionary pioneers in the field of bones and spinal cords. From their first experiments along these lines, about 45 million years ago, they developed themselves from jawless, lobe-finned creatures plodding along the muddy seafloor to such noble specimens as the marlin and the rainbow trout. While thus engaged in their biological ascendancy, many of the earlier models of fish perished along the way. Some of the ancient ones, however, have survived relatively unchanged to this very day. These elders include the coelecanth, the lungfish, several primitive varieties of sharks and rays . . . and gars. Gars have been around for a mighty long time. Gar watched the dinosaurs rise and fall and witnessed the ancient tropical forests turn into beds of coal. There were probably gar frolicking in the wake of Noah's Ark.

Although fossil forms have been found in the rocks of Europe and India, the gar of the present era are strictly Western Hemisphere residents. They are found throughout much of the United States and up into southern Canada, as well as in Cuba and parts of mainland South America. There are several species, all fairly similar in appearance: a long, streamlined body (the word "gar" comes from the Anglo-Saxon term for a spear or lance), a hard bony beak full of sharp teeth, and ganoid scales. These are a primitive type, theorized to be the transitional form between modern scales and the armor-like coating of bygone stages in the history of fish. The tough, diamond-shaped plates fit together like a medieval knight's coat of chain mail. Gar scales were sometimes made into arrowheads by Indian tribes who had no flint or other suitable minerals available.

Although providing excellent protection from scrapes and puncture wounds, this protective covering limits the flexibility of its owners; gar are not as spry and limber as most fish. I once watched an alligator gar in a large aquarium trying to eat a small live carp that had been provided for its supper. The gar would charge at its intended victim at full speed, only to have it do the aquatic equivalent of a side-step out of the way. Its inability to bend would cause the gar to shoot straight past the carp, like a bull fooled by a matador's cape. In the wild, gars avoid this problem by hiding in thick vegetation until a likely meal swims by. If ambushed quickly enough, the prey fish won't have time for evasive action.

Gars are classified in the genera *Lepisosteus* and *Atractosteus*. The two are similar in overall appearance, but there are slight structural differences. The most noticeable of these is that the *Lepisosteus* gars only have one row of teeth in their upper jaws, while those of the *Atractosteus* persuasion have two.

The shortnose gar (*L. platostomus*) is the pipsqueak of the family—maybe a yard long and weighing three to four pounds. As might be deduced from its common name, it has a relatively short snout.

The spotted gar (*L. oculatus*) looks a lot like the shortnose but has round black spots on top of the head, snout, and body. It, too, reaches a maximum length of about three feet but gets a little chunkier than the shortnose, sometimes up to ten pounds.

The longnose gar (*L. osseus*) gets bigger yet (and not just its nose; the whole fish). Specimens exceeding three feet long are fairly common, and they can tip the scales at over twenty-five pounds. Obviously, they have a long, narrow snout.

Then we have the Big Daddy of the tribe: *Atractosteus spatula*, the alligator gar. This is a big, really big, virtually Texas-sized, fish, up to ten feet long. The current record, caught on a trotline in the Rio Grande, weighed three hundred and two pounds.

Many people, including some who really should know better, say that the alligator gar is a trash fish. By this they mean that it has no "value": not suitable for sport, not good to eat, and they eat other fish. This is largely untrue. Alligator gar make for excellent sport, particularly when hunted with a bow and arrow or a harpoon. It's true that they're difficult to land with a rod and reel; their hard bony mouths don't set a hook well. The flesh of the alligator gar is not only nontoxic (it's sometimes believed to be poisonous if eaten—total nonsense), it's delicious. And as far as eating other fish...Well, that's what fish do for a living. As Shakespeare put it, they live as do men; the larger fall upon the smaller. Recent studies have shown, however, that much of the alligator gar's diet consists of other "rough fish" that are not usually sought for either sport or human consumption.

The alligator gar is relatively common in Texas, especially in the eastern two-thirds of the state. Fishermen who believe that nonsense about gar being inedible will often go out of their way to kill them, and the population may be declining due to this. On a past fishing trip to the Trinity River, I came across a fairly large, and just about dead, alligator gar floating listlessly on the surface. Closer examination of the pitiful creature revealed that someone had wired its jaws shut and turned it loose to starve to death. I had no way of knowing exactly how long it had been suffering this way, but the skin had already grown over the wire. Unfortunately, there are sadistic perverts found among every sampling of society, including fishermen.

The recent rise in popularity of bow fishing has actually been a good thing for the alligator gar. Bow fishermen are about the only sizable group in the state who actually want this fish around, and every species needs somebody to stick up for it. A few people also pursue the alligator gar with rod and reel or trotline tactics. The preferred method is to attach some live bait to a tangled ball of monofilament line or frayed rope, so that the strands snag in the gar's teeth; otherwise it probably couldn't be landed.

Prior to invasion of its territory by the human race, the alligator gar was pretty much the lord and master of the Texas freshwaters. Millions of years of practice had endowed the fish with considerable survival skills, and there wasn't too much it had to fear. Very young gar can be preyed upon occasionally by the normal eaters of fish—storks, snapping turtles, ospreys, bigger fish (including their own parents)—but even these would rather eat something softer if given the choice. Once maturity is obtained, the huge armored body and mouth full of razor-sharp teeth discourage attack from just about anything except full-grown alligators and crocodiles. I once read a report that portions of a large gar were found in the stomach of a shark landed in Florida, but this is probably an unusual situation. Alligator gars do occasionally venture out into the sea, but they don't make it a regular habit.

Some scientists consider the alligator gar as a sort of "bridge species" between fish and the reptile/amphibian group. Whether or not this is correct, it's undeniable that this fish has a few characteristics that are decidedly unfishy. As mentioned earlier, the scales are different from those of most others. The skeletal structure is unusual: The vertebrae have a ball-and-socket structure similar to that found in some reptiles. The dorsal fin sits far back on the heavily scaled body, and the swim bladder—in most fish, a bag of gas for buoyancy control—has a system of blood vessels that enable it to function as a primitive lung. Although gills are more efficient than lungs as a general rule (they are able to extract about eighty-five percent of the oxygen from water; lungs can only extract around twenty-five percent from air), the function is limited. Most fish cannot survive in stagnant, oxygen-depleted waters. In a situation where trout and bass would soon suffocate and go belly-up, the gar needn't worry; it just sticks its ugly head above the surface and gulps in some air.

Many years ago, the story goes, a Cherokee Indian boy caught a baby alligator gar and decided to keep it for a pet. He put his new companion in a hollow stump filled with rainwater and fed it daily on minnows and tadpoles he scooped from the shallows. As the fish grew, he continually transferred it to larger living quarters. Eventually he couldn't find any hollow stumps big enough to hold it and was forced to return the gar to a nearby pond. By this time the two had bonded for life, however. Whenever the lad came to the shores of the pond and whistled, his scaly sidekick would haul its now-considerable bulk up on the shore to be scratched and petted. Sometimes it would even initiate the visit on its own, leaving the water entirely and dragging itself through the wet grass to the Cherokee village. The inhabitants had grown quite fond of their unusual "mascot" and would often feed it the scraps from their meals. Sometimes the village children would ride on its back.

One summer there was a severe drought, and the gar's home pond grew smaller by the day. It soon became little more than a mud hole, but the gar by this time had grown accustomed to breathing air on a regular basis and didn't suffer too greatly. Whenever the owner—now a strapping young warrior—came to visit, he'd find his friend dozing in the mud, like some gigantic misshapen hog. The familiar whistle of greeting would catch the gar's attention. It always opened its enormous mouth in a toothy grin and made a valiant attempt to wag its armored tail.

The man and his gar sometimes entered the woods on hunting expeditions together. The fish had become quite adept at sliding through the underbrush and could even haul itself over fallen logs. As its appetite increased with its size, the gar was often required to catch its own food. This it did by concealing itself in the bushes and springing out on unwary rabbits and possums. Eventually it even took full-grown deer, and on particularly successful days it would bring one back to share with its human friends. The gar was sometimes a better hunter than the men of the village, but it had an extra advantage in this respect. Any deer that scented a human in the vicinity would tend to be on its guard. The smell of a fish wasn't considered any cause for worry. One big buck, on seeing the monstrous gar charge out from the foliage, had actually died of surprise before the fish even reached it.

The village children were playing by the riverbank one sunny morning, frolicking in the shallows and splashing each other with water. One of these cheerful youngsters was the beautiful daughter of the man who, many years earlier, had brought the baby gar home for a pet. She was having such a good time playing with her friends that she failed to notice the dark, log-like shape of an alligator approaching the shallows. The big reptile lunged and snapped at the little girl. It missed her legs but snagged her buckskin skirt on one of its teeth and began to drag her into the river. Quite naturally, she screamed with fright, and as her playmates realized what was happening, they began to scream as well. One brave young lad picked up a stick and began to beat the alligator with it, but to no effect.

Suddenly there was a tremendous crashing through the woods of the riverbank, and the village gar came charging out at full speed. Sharp teeth gnashing in its cavernous mouth, its red eyes blazing with anger, it shot down the muddy bank and into the shallows, ramming the alligator broadside with such force that the little girl was jarred loose. Into the center of the river went the two combatants, the huge reptile and the equally huge fish, their frenzied fighting churning the water into a bloody froth. It was nip and tuck for several minutes until the gar managed to get its enormous jaws around the alligator's midsection and bit it completely in half.

Although the little girl was saved and the alligator destroyed, the ending of this story isn't a completely happy one. The heroic gar, you see, had been living on land for so long that it had forgotten how to swim—so it drowned.

As a general rule, of course, most alligator gars live out their lives in an aquatic environment. The preferred habitat is a somewhat protected pocket of slow-flowing water, with lots of weeds or moss beds to provide cover. Gar can generally be found wherever other "rough fish"—carp, drum, etc.—are encountered.

The alligator gar spawns in groups, usually in areas of thick underwater vegetation. The greenish eggs are poisonous to many creatures, including humans, which gives them a somewhat higher survival rate than the roe of many other species (there will never be any market for gar caviar!). This characteristic of the eggs leads many people to assume that the flesh of the mature gar is also poisonous, but as mentioned earlier, this is a fallacy.

The fish grows rapidly, sometimes exceeding twenty inches in length by its first birthday. Naturally, the growth rate is determined by the available food supply. A well-nourished fish will always grow faster than a hungry one. The maximum length seems to be about ten feet. (I've heard unsubstantiated tales of twenty-footers, but then, I also heard the story about the one that saved the little girl from the alligator. I take both these tales with a bit of skepticism, and I hope you do too.). Once a suitable length is reached, the alligator gar begins to bulk up, its girth expanding until it takes on the appearance of a floating log.

The most popular method of bagging an alligator gar is with the use of a bow-fishing rig. There's no need for fancy equipment; just about any bow with a reel adapter will suffice. Being an optimist, I've always used 200-lb. test line when I've gone gar hunting, but my luck has never been good enough to justify it. Whether fishing with bow or with rod and reel, I never seem to get a chance at the real whoppers. Landing a sizable gar with an arrow on a line isn't quite as easy as it might sound to the uninitiated. Besides finding a big one, which like all fishing is mostly a matter of chance, a lot can happen between the sighting and the hauling in. If the arrow doesn't strike the target just right, it's liable to bounce off of the tough scales harmlessly. Even when proper penetration is achieved, the quarry often escapes either by snagging up the line until it breaks, or through pure brute strength. Unless a vital spot is hit, the alligator gar usually heals its wounds rapidly.

Although fair-sized gar can frequently be found during the day, night fishing is often preferred. The really big fish seem to spend a lot of their daylight hours dozing in the weeds and do the bulk of their feeding after sundown. If you aim a spotlight at a floating log and see a couple of eyes reflecting back at you, you've most likely found yourself a gar or, depending on the area, an alligator. Be sure of what you've come across before you take a shot at it, both for your own safety and for respect of the game laws.

Jug line fishing—a baited hook suspended from a float—is another method of bringing home an alligator gar. Depending on the size of the gar being sought, anything from a gallon milk jug to an empty oil drum may be utilized as a float. Some fishermen use a brace of crossed two-by-fours to hopefully hang up the hooked gar in a brushy area. If a really big one takes the bait, the float may simply never be seen again.

The meat of an alligator gar is good eating, despite prevalent rumors to the contrary. I often come across printed passages such as the following: (I won't name the source, as I don't want to embarrass the author, who seems to be basically a decent fellow.) "[Gar] have no value as a food fish because their flesh tastes so bad that few people are willing to eat it."

Well, all I can say is that the writer of that line either never tasted alligator gar, or whoever cooked it for him did a really poor job of it. Although the white meat is crumbly—you'll never get a decent-sized filet from a gar—it's both tasty and nutritious. I have two main methods of cooking gar, the Cajun style and the Mexican style.

Before either recipe is used, you first have to separate the meat from the rest of the gar. If your fish is of any size to make this task worthwhile, it calls for a sharp hatchet (or a chainsaw). Put the chunks of meat thus obtained into a suitable container (dishpan, bucket, washtub, or whatever the quantity calls for) until all that remains is bones, scales, and teeth. Save the scales for making arrowheads if you wish.

Cajun cuisine calls for mixing the meat with cornmeal (for its binding properties) and whatever seasonings tickle the cook's palate. Garlic, onion, and cayenne pepper are the common choices, in proportions determined by personal taste. Form this mixture into patties and deep-fry them; the results are delicious! These patties are commonly called "gar balls" in East Texas and Louisiana, often a source of some consternation to those who are sampling them for the first time.

For the Mexican style of preparation, the pan/bucket/washtub of gar meat is transferred to an appropriately sized pot. Stewed with onions, potatoes, green chili, and cilantro; served with warm tortillas and a cold beer—who could ask for a better meal to cap off a day of bow fishing?

By action of the State Legislature, the Guadalupe bass is the official fish of Texas. Nothing really wrong with that, I guess. The Guadalupe bass is a pretty decent game fish for rod and reel sportsmen and good to eat as well. But had it been up to me, I would have chosen the alligator gar, by virtue of its great size, its even greater antiquity, and, yes, its personality. Sure, it moves a little slow most of the time; so what? It can swim fast when it takes a mind to; it just doesn't take a mind to all that often. In this age of excessive speed and stressfully paced living, I think the alligator gar can serve as an example to all of us to take things a little more easily now and then.

CHAPTER SIXTEEN

The Whooping Crane

The whooping crane (*Grus americana*) is probably the best-known success story of the entire American conservation movement. The bird itself could not have been designed any better as a symbol for a group to rally around. It's big, it's beautiful, it's majestic, and it doesn't eat people or damage their crops. Both its original range of distribution and its total population were drastically reduced through human intervention (almost, but not quite, to the point of no return) right at a period of history when the average American was just beginning to give a damn about such things. Like I said, perfect.

Of course, the whooping crane's future is still not completely secure, and there's a good chance that it never will be. A lot of people tend to blame the endangerment of a once-hunted species solely on hunting and are under the impression that "protection" from human predation will solve the problem. Not so. The whooping crane was probably never very numerous to begin with (it's estimated that there were only about two thousand of them when Europeans first reached the New World) and its biggest problem is the spread of civilization in general. Development and pollution of its natural habitat, particularly the draining of wetlands, has done more damage to the population than hunters ever could.

Not that hunting didn't put a dent in the numbers, of course. Whooping cranes had grown accustomed to being relatively safe from human predation—their sharp eyesight and quick reflexes were more than a match for the slings and arrows of Pre-Columbian hunters—and consequently were not nearly as afraid of humans as they should have been. The introduction of firearms caught these big birds completely by surprise. It took a couple of generations of exposure to this new technology before they realized that a man could kill a whooping crane from quite some distance away. Interestingly, the earliest reference to the whooping crane I've discovered (1722) stated only that they could be used to make "an excellent soup."

Cranes in general have always had a strong effect on the human imagination, perhaps because cranes sometimes seem very human-like in their behavior and mannerisms. With the possible exception of penguins, I can't think of any bird that walks more like a man—a lanky and somewhat awkward man, admittedly, but the resemblance is definitely there.

Throughout the world, wherever cranes are found, a body of folklore has grown up around them. As a general rule cranes are associated with peace or good fortune, but in parts of the American South it was once believed that if a crane circled above a house three times, it signified an impending death among the residents. Such beliefs are hard to invalidate, as people are constantly dying for one reason or another. If, at some time during anyone's memory, a crane had happened to circle the deceased's home three times, this was considered "proof."

The Ancient Greeks seem to have started the legend that cranes post sentinels around a resting flock to warn the others of danger, and that these sentinels keep one foot raised with a stone clutched in their toes. Should the bird on guard duty start to fall asleep at its post, it will be awakened by the falling stone. In the Middle Ages, this story frequently turned up as a Christian parable: We should be as watchful as the cranes and use our faith as a stone to warn us against the dangers of falling into sinful behavior.

The "whooper" is the largest of American cranes, standing about five feet high when fully grown, and with a wingspan often exceeding seven feet. Like most flying birds, whooping cranes are a lot lighter than they look. A big male will tip the scales at about fifteen or sixteen pounds. It's an attractive species, almost entirely white, with black wing tips and a bright red patch of unfeathered skin on the head.

All cranes of the genus *Grus*, including the American sandhill crane and the saurus crane of Asia and Australia, have an unusually long trachea (windpipe) coiled up like a French horn inside the hollow of the breastbone. This anatomical peculiarity is what enables the birds to produce such loud, resonating calls, and the whooping crane produces the loudest and most resonating call of them all—hence the name. Early settlers to North America apparently felt that the sound was similar to an Indian "war whoop."

Although the total population was never large, what whooping cranes there were formerly bred across much of the continent. The original range seems to have been from central Canada through the Midwestern United States to the Gulf of Mexico. Most were migratory, spending the warmer months (when they bred and nested) in the North Plains, then coming down to the Gulf Coast for the winter. A small resident population seems to have remained in East Texas and Louisiana year round.

As the virgin prairies of the U.S. and Canada became wheat fields and cow pastures, the cranes pushed their breeding grounds into more remote areas. Whooping cranes vanished from Illinois by 1880 and from North Dakota and Minnesota within a few more years. The last ones known to nest in the United States were found in Iowa during the 1890s. In 1922 a breeding pair with a nestling was discovered in Saskatchewan, and it was immediately "collected" (in other words, shot and stuffed) for a Canadian museum. After this, no one knew where the migratory population reared their offspring. This was probably fortunate for the remaining birds, as they no doubt would have been "collected."

Meanwhile, the Southern branch of the family was having problems of its own. The main reason these nonmigrating cranes had managed to hang on for as long as they had was because they lived in remote and largely inaccessible coastal marshes. When the U.S. Army Corps of Engineers extended the Intracoastal Waterway in the late 1920s, these areas were no longer so remote and inaccessible. They were soon planted with rice and sugar cane. The change in the neighborhood didn't agree with the whooping cranes, and by 1940 there were only six left in the area.

The migrants, although reduced to fifteen known individuals, continued to spend their winters on the Texas coast. In 1937 the Bureau of Biological Survey (later to become the U.S. Fish and Wildlife Service) established a seventy-five-acre preserve on the Blackjack Peninsula. Every autumn the whooping cranes would materialize out of the skies and spend several months in their newly protected habitat. They would happily settle in for the season, relaxing in the warm Texas sunshine and waxing fat and happy on a diet of fish, frogs, crawdads, and the occasional rattlesnake.

Today that habitat is the Aransas National Wildlife Refuge. I've been fortunate enough to be there when the cranes began to arrive, and I thank God and the Bureau of Biological Survey that the species was saved. I was born too late to see passenger pigeons or great auks, but at least I've seen the whooping cranes—an experience to remember. They begin as specks of white in the distant sky, looking like leftover scraps of tattered clouds, then gradually grow larger and take the form of big, magnificent birds. And, of course, they whoop.

It's now common knowledge that the whooping cranes nest and breed in Wood Buffalo Park, eleven million acres of Canadian wilderness originally established for the benefit of (what else?) the wood buffalo. Finding this out was no easy task, however. For many years the breeding ground of the whooping crane was the Holy Grail of ornithology. Its whereabouts remained unknown though eagerly sought by many a valiant crusader.

American conservationists were determined to find out where the whooping cranes spent their summers. Primarily, this was for the purpose of protecting it from development; secondarily they just wanted to know. Naturalists are an inquisitive breed, and they hate being in the dark about such matters.

In 1945 the U.S. Fish and Wildlife Service and the National Audubon Society joined forces to create the Cooperative Whooping Crane Project. Their mission was to sponsor research on the biology of the species, with the highest priority given to finding those breeding grounds. As more and more of the general public became interested in whooping cranes, the fact that nobody knew where they nested was becoming a point of major scientific embarrassment.

First to take up the quest was Fred Bard, a museum zoologist from Regina, Saskatchewan. Assisted by U.S. wildlife biologist Robert Smith, Bard spent the spring and summer of 1945 searching through western Canada for whooping crane nests. The team drew a blank. The next breeding season, the torch was passed to Dr. O.S. Pettingill, with Smith continuing to help out. Once again the search proved fruitless. When Pettingill returned to his teaching position in the autumn of 1946, Robert Porter Allen took over the quest. Unlike his predecessors, Allen absolutely refused to give up. Every winter he studied the whooping cranes in Texas, observing every possible detail of their natural history. Every summer he searched for their breeding grounds in Canada.

With the technology available today, tracking down the whoopers would have been a piece of cake. A few of the birds would have been fitted with electronic tracking devices while wintering on the Gulf, and their entire migration route, including the precise geographic coordinates of the final destination, could have been printed out on a computer screen. For Robert Allen, the task was not quite so simple. It meant many seasons of hiking over thousands of square miles of soggy tundra; of paddling canoes up and down countless rivers, and the backbreaking task of portaging those canoes and other equipment around rapids and log jams. It meant being eaten alive by hordes of mosquitoes and biting flies while following up on every possible lead offered by hunters and trappers who had glimpsed a "big white bird" in the area. I never met Robert Allen, but I admire the man tremendously. I sometimes wonder if anyone else could have measured up to the task.

The greatest search in the history of conservation finally came to a climax in 1955. A month into his annual pilgrimage to the barrens, Allen recorded in his journal: "It has taken us 31 days and a lot of grief, but let it be known that at 2 p.m. on this 23rd day of June, we are on the ground with the Whooping Cranes! We have finally made it!"

Another interesting chapter in the saga of the whooping crane concerns the adventures of two birds originally christened "Pete" and "Joe." During the 1930s, when the whooping crane population was at one of its lowest points, Pete was found tangled in a barbed wire fence in Nebraska. He was in pretty sorry shape: exhausted, half-starved, one eye shot out, and a broken wing. A boy rescued the unfortunate crane and delivered it by bicycle to a local surgeon who saved the crane's life. For the next fourteen years Pete lived a life of misery as a captive of the Nebraska Rod and Gun Club. Unable to fly, he was kept in a fenced enclosure and fed on whatever scraps and garbage the curious visitors tossed into his pen.

Joe, meanwhile, had allegedly been caught in a muskrat trap in Louisiana. His sojourn in the civilized world was at least as bad as Pete's: Confined to a concrete-floored cage, his feet—designed for, and accustomed to, wading through soft mud—developed crippling lesions. Joe was quite literally on his last legs when he and Pete were released in a large natural enclosure on the Texas refuge in October of 1948. As neither of them were able to fly, they involuntarily became the first permanent residents in several years.

It was fervently hoped that Joe and Pete would respond to a suitable diet and habitat, as well as to the sound and sight of other whooping cranes (the migrants) around them. It was also fervently hoped that one of them was male and one of them was female. At that time there was no way short of an autopsy to find out. Joe and Pete seemed to get along with each other well enough, but no romantic overtures were observed.

Another disabled and nonflying whooper known as "Old Crip" was later introduced into the same enclosure. This newcomer was assumed to be a male, due to his great size (he was supposedly the biggest one the refuge managers had ever seen). The initial results of this operation seemed encouraging: Pete spent all of his time trying to run Old Crip off, while Joe coyly watched from a distance. The logical assumption, of course, was that Pete and Old Crip were both males. "Joe" was taken to be the lady of the bunch and subsequently renamed "Josephine."

The refuge personnel had wisely provided the whooping cranes with lots of room (and lots of privacy) to let nature take its course and so were unable to document everything that happened during the birds' relationship. However, on May 4, 1949, a nest containing two eggs was found in the enclosure. Further observation of the pair, compared with past records of the behavior of whooping crane couples, led to a change of opinion among the scientists assigned to the case. It was now believed that "Pete" had laid the eggs, so she became "Petunia" while "Josephine" reverted to "Joe."

Unfortunately, the magic seemed to have somehow gone out of the relationship. Later in the month of May, the formerly happy couple began ignoring their potential offspring. Later still, they deliberately destroyed both nest and eggs; but examination of the remains showed that the eggs had been infertile anyway. Were both of the captive whoopers female? Some opinions leaned in that direction. However, it had already been established that up to thirty percent of the eggs of the sandhill crane (*Grus canadensis*, the whooping crane's closest relative) are infertile. Did the same ratio apply to whooping crane eggs? The mystery remained unsolved.

On May 25 an apparent sexual encounter between the two cranes was observed for the first time, but it only added to the confusion. Pete/Petunia was seen to take the male role and mount Joe/Josephine, who didn't put up any protest about it, even crouching down in the normal way of a receptive member of the feminine persuasion. According to the eyewitnesses—R.W. Clapper of the refuge staff and naturalist Roy Bedichek—the union was never actually consummated. In those days it wasn't necessary for the media to be politically correct, and reports of the incident hinted at an "unnatural relationship."

On July 22, 1949, Pete/Petunia passed away in the night, apparently of natural causes. Joe/Josephine was reported to have wailed continuously from about one in the morning until sunrise, then intermittently throughout the day. This was supposedly a quite different call from the normal whooping that gave the birds their name. It was described as both "monotonous" and "mournful." Can a whooping crane understand the loss of a loved one and mourn accordingly? Do non-human—even non-mammalian—species feel the emotion we know as "sorrow" at the death of a companion? Maybe, maybe not; but the evidence would seem to indicate that at least one whooping crane felt that emotion all too well.

As it turned out, Pete really had been Pete all along. An autopsy performed at the Patuxent Research Refuge (Maryland) removed any doubt as to the maleness of his gender. Of course, this also proved that Joe was Josephine, because somebody had to have laid those eggs.

Old Crip was now back in the picture. He had been living the bachelor life in a marshy area about ten miles from the experimental enclosure, which the widowed Josephine now occupied alone. The refuge staff brought Old Crip out of retirement, washed his face and combed his hair, and sent him out a-courtin'. Josephine seemed to accept his company gracefully. As of yet, no one was actually positive that Crip was a male, but once again hopes were raised.

On May 26, 1950, the first whooping crane ever hatched in captivity (and at the time, the thirty-eighth member of its species known to exist) was seen to emerge from a patch of cattails in Crip and Josephine's enclosure. Like all baby whoopers, this one was a dingy reddish-brown, and they named it "Rusty." Old Crip apparently still had what it takes.

In the decades following this grand experiment, other methods of increasing the whooping crane's numbers have been tried. Most of these involved pilfering an egg from the nest. Whoopers usually produce two eggs but only manage to raise one of the hatchlings, so the extra eggs have been artificially incubated. Captive flocks were established at both the Patuxent Research Center and the International Crane Foundation in Wisconsin.

Beginning in 1975, attempts were made to place whooping crane eggs in the nests of sandhill cranes, but this has been largely unsuccessful. Although the sandhills showed no apparent reluctance to rear these foundlings as their own, the mission seemed to have met with a lot of bad luck right from the start. Most of the eggs or hatchlings were lost due to various natural causes such as flooding or coyote predation. The few foster whooping cranes that survived never attempted to breed among themselves. It was suspected that these birds had become "imprinted" with the idea that they were sandhill cranes themselves and therefore had no clue that they were supposed to mate with other whooping cranes. The egg transfer project was finally abandoned in 1989.

Of course, I'm setting myself up for accusations of flagrant Texanism here, but in my opinion the ones that winter at Aransas are the only real whooping cranes. It's just that, to me, there is an obvious difference between an animal that lives out its life in the natural environment for which it was created, and a member of the same species that grows up elsewhere, whether pampered and hand-fed or abused and neglected. The first leopard I ever saw was a mangy, toothless, pitiful old specimen in a filthy cage. Years later I was introduced to another one: a flabby, obese "exotic pet" that spent its days lounging on a foam rubber mattress, dining on chicken gravy and canned salmon. Many more years later, I saw a leopard pounce on an antelope almost its own size, kill it with a bite through the neck, and haul the carcass fifteen feet up an acacia tree. Zoologically speaking, all three of these were leopards, but only the last one was a real leopard.

In the same way, the Aransas flock is made up of the real whooping cranes. Appearing at the coastal marshes after flying thousands of miles, staking out their designated family territories and dueling among themselves to defend them, teaching their young how to stalk and spear unwary frogs... This is how the birds were meant to live. In the early spring they grow restless and begin to circle higher and higher above their winter feeding grounds. Eventually they feel the full effect of whatever instinctive force calls them back north, and they return to the wilderness past Great Slave Lake. I consider myself fortunate to have witnessed this. The whooping crane came much too close to going the way of the passenger pigeon, the great auk, and the dodo. I was born too late to have seen any of these birds as anything other than pictures, and I can only hope that none of my descendants are in the same situation concerning the whooping crane.

CHAPTER SEVENTEEN

The Weevil and the Worm

Most non-Texans (and even some natives) think that cattle and crude oil are the most important products of the Lone Star State. Although both of these do, indeed, play a major role in the regional economy, the real star of the show is cotton. During any given year, four to five million acres of Texas are devoted to growing cotton, and when you take into consideration the other industrial bases that depend on this crop (textile plants, shipping companies, manufacturers and maintainers of agricultural machinery, etc.) it becomes obvious that cotton is still king. Cattle ranching has a more colorful heritage, and oil wells have made more individuals wealthy in a hurry, but as far as putting food on the table, more families depend on cotton than any other commodity in the state.

The historical basis for this favored cash crop is based on simple economics. Just about anybody in the Texas of the previous century could manage to buy, or at least sharecrop, enough land to make a little profit with cotton. Going into the cattle business required a much larger initial investment. As the years passed, however, many people raised cotton simply because raising cotton seemed to be the thing to do. As it was once put by Clarence Ousley of the U.S. Department of Agriculture: "The psychology of growing and selling cotton is almost a mania. I have frequently said that I do not know whether cotton is a plant or a mental disease."

Unfortunately for the humans who live off this crop, a number of other species try to do likewise. Insects of many shapes and sizes are the cotton grower's worst nemesis. Even a casual glance at any agricultural textbook will reveal a long list of "bad bugs." There are seedling thrips and whiteflies, aphids and stinkbugs and fleahoppers. There are cutworms, bollworms, leafworms, and army worms. Cotton is even attacked by insects that more commonly feed on other crops—the tobacco budworm, cabbage looper, and corn borer, for example. It seems as though a field of cotton is a veritable beacon to every hungry insect for miles around. There may as well be a flashing neon sign reading "Free Lunch."

One of the better-known villains in this scenario is the boll weevil, one of the few insects immortalized in song.

> *Well, de boll weevil am a little black bug,*
> *come from Mexico, dey say.*
> *Come all de way to Texas,*
> *jes' a-lookin' fo' a place to stay.*
> *Jes' a-lookin' fo' a home,*
> *jes' a-lookin' fo' a home.*

This old folk ditty, traditionally performed in Uncle Remus dialect, pretty much sums up the early history of the boll weevil. It did, indeed, find itself a home—first in Texas, then throughout much of the rest of the country. Wherever cotton was grown, the boll weevil (*Anthonomus grandis*) soon put in an unwelcome appearance. Entire plantations were sometimes devastated by boll weevils. Of course, as the saying goes, there's a good side to just about everything, and the boll weevil was no exception. Its ravages on the cotton fields forced farmers in many areas to diversify their lands with other crops, and in the long run this became an economic advantage (as well as an environmental one). In fact, a monument to the boll weevil was erected in the town square of Enterprise, Alabama, in appreciation of its role in opening the local farmers' eyes to this concept.

There are lots of types of weevils in the world, of which the boll is merely one. Weevils, in general, are beetles with long, curved snouts. (This feature, plus their buggy eyes, make them somewhat resemble the "Gonzo" character from Jim Henson's

Muppets.) Their propensity for feeding on rather specialized diets accounts for their common names: bean weevil, palm weevil, rice weevil, etc. The boll weevil, quite naturally, eats cotton bolls. In its natural state, it was found only in central Mexico, where it spent a low-profile existence feeding on wild cotton. It was first scientifically classified about 1830 and was considered to be rather rare.

The boll weevil didn't stay rare for long. Cotton farming soon caught on in Mexico in a big way, and the little black bug took full advantage of the situation. By 1880 it was considered a serious agricultural pest South of the Border, and in 1892 it crossed the Rio Grande jes' a-lookin' for a home. In 1903 it was in Louisiana; it reached Oklahoma, Arkansas, and Mississippi in 1907. By 1920 the entire Cotton Belt was thoroughly infested, and the human population of the region wasn't a bit happy about it.

The natural history of *A. grandis* seems perfectly designed to make it a serious pest. For one thing, it's capable of flying relatively great distances in search of its next meal—up to a hundred miles or so, with favorable wind conditions. Uncultivated areas and bodies of water are consequently no great barriers to its expansion. Additionally, adult boll weevils are incredibly prolific. Each female can lay several hundred eggs per season (and, at only two or three eggs per boll, that accounts for a lot of ruined cotton). Growth and maturity are rapid, allowing multiple generations per year; it only takes one pregnant weevil in the patch to start a major infestation.

The long, slender snout of the boll weevil is used to puncture the developing cotton boll. A couple of eggs are then laid in the opening, and the maggot-like larvae feed on the inside, eventually hollowing it out. When they pupate (enter their cocoon stage) their bodies release a chemical enzyme that causes the cotton boll to open prematurely, rot, and fall off. A week or so after this, the now-grown weevils emerge from the ruined boll, find mates, and repeat the process.

In areas where it's warm the year around, the boll weevil carries on its destructive lifestyle the year around as well. When cold weather occurs, adult weevils enter a state of semi-hibernation, hiding in leaf litter or burrowing into the roots of the cotton plants. Come the spring, they emerge and begin the cycle again.

Until fairly recently, the only reaction to any unwelcome insects in the fields was to saturate the area with as much poison as the particular farmer could afford to buy (and, sadly, this still happens in some places). Although this process barely put a dent in the boll weevil population, it took a serious toll of horned toads, prairie chickens, and other insect-eating wildlife. It then traveled up the food chain to hawks, bobcats, and larger predators. Runoff from the toxic fields polluted the waterways, killing fish, shrimp, oysters, and pelicans.

Today, the IPM (Integrated Pest Management) Program is carried out in most cotton-producing regions. Although pesticides are still used—thankfully, in moderation for the most part—IPM calls primarily for breaking the weevil's reproductive cycle. Crop rotation is practiced, and old cotton fields are intensively cultivated to destroy the overwintering weevils. The problem is far from over and probably never will be, but boll weevils are now under enough control to keep the price of cotton at an affordable level (and the farmers from starving to death).

Although it never had a song composed in its honor (at least I've never heard one), the pink bollworm's story is just as interesting. *Pectinophora gossypiella*, in its adult form, is a small (total wingspan less than one inch), insignificant-looking, dark brown moth. Today it is found throughout North and South America but is actually native to the Old World. Its exact place of origin is a matter of speculation; many believe it to be the Mediterranean region. It is thought to have been inadvertently imported into Mexico from Egypt about 1910.

The larva of this little moth is the stage of its life history that most interests humans, for, like the boll weevil, it destroys cotton. A female moth lays about a hundred eggs per season, spreading them out among four or five different cotton bolls. It only takes about a week or so for these to hatch into pinkish larvae and begin feeding on their host plant, destroying the boll in the process and consequently preventing the formation of any cotton fibers. After a month as a half-inch long caterpillar, the insect spends another month as a pupa in a cocoon, then emerges to live yet another month as a moth. With such an accelerated life span, it doesn't take long for a couple of tiny dark moths to become an entire cotton patch of hungry pink caterpillars. As if this weren't bad enough, the creature seems capable, when necessary, of "suspending" itself as a pupa should the weather turn cold. Instead of the normal thirty days spent in the cocoon, it may remain in such a stage for two years or more until it somehow senses conditions are favorable for its emergence. Unlike many other alien insect invaders, which are totally adapted to tropical climates, the pink bollworm can thus survive through the longest of American winters.

When the first pink bollworm in Texas was discovered in a cotton field near Hearne, it sparked something of a panic throughout the Lone Star State. This was in September of 1917, less than two decades following the attack of the boll weevil, from which the cotton industry was finally starting to recover. The very last thing the farmers of Texas wanted was yet another exotic cotton pest on the rampage.

Unfortunately, those who grew the cotton feared the government's reaction to the bollworm nearly as much as they feared the bollworm itself. The initial plan was to set up a series of strictly enforced "no cotton" zones along the Mexican border. All existing cotton plants would be plowed up and burned and no new crops allowed to be planted. No doubt this idea seemed perfectly feasible to many people, but not, of course, to those who made a living by growing cotton within the prospective quarantined areas. For them, it would have been the Kiss of Death. Many farmers preferred to take their chances with the worm (they looked at it more as just the Kiss of Serious Injury). An alternative plan was to somehow impose the "no-cotton" zone on the other side of the Rio Grande, but the farmers of Mexico weren't any more receptive to this idea than had been the farmers of Texas. As in most cases of this sort, the control measures were accepted as reasonable by everybody except the people who would be subject to those controls.

Cooperation with Mexico to fight the pink bollworm was difficult. The year 1917 was a particularly tumultuous year for our neighbor to the south. Pancho Villa and Emiliano Zapata were stirring up revolution and had as many, if not more, active followers than the current "official" government. The semianarchic conditions prevailing through most of the nation had spawned the rise of numerous local warlords and bandito chieftains, each ruling his own little empire. All things considered, it was not a very good time for any American scientists to travel in rural Mexico looking for insects.

The United States government had its own plate fairly full with the little matter of World War I. Despite this, sufficient federal funds (about $500,000 by the end of it all) were scraped together to take action against the pink bollworm. The biggest share of this was earmarked for new inspection stations and fumigation facilities along the Mexican border. No doubt these helped somewhat. Infested cottonseed was kept from entering the country, and railroad cars that may have contained eggs or larvae were effectively sanitized. However, the adult stage of the pink bollworm is, as you recall, a moth, and moths can fly. The chances of them adjusting their flight patterns to pass through the government checkpoints were unlikely.

So, despite the government's efforts at closing the border to it, the pink bollworm established itself in Texas. Over the next few years it turned up in various locations along the Rio Grande, and, eventually, in the Galveston area. This particular population was blamed on the hurricane of 1915. In August of that year, 27,000 bales of cotton—much of it from Mexico—had been lost at sea, and remnants of the cargo had washed ashore at various points along the coast. Had there been bollworm infestation in any of this cotton, some would probably have survived.

Texas was in a hard spot now. The U.S. government was seriously considering placing a ban on all Texas cotton, which would have been a major economic disaster for the state. Florida had already passed its own local regulations prohibiting the import of Texas cotton, and it looked as though other states might soon follow suit.

The agricultural scientists and political leaders of Texas were doing everything within their respective powers to prevent such an occurrence. Quarantine zones were established where cotton was forbidden to be grown for the next three years. Thousands of acres of bollworm-infested cotton were plowed up and burned and the fields cleaned to a microscopic level. (One observer reported a former cotton plantation to be "swept clean as a city street." Of course, back then city streets were much cleaner than they usually are today.) Agricultural agents trained in spotting signs of bollworm presence wandered the back roads of cotton country with literal *carte blanche* to order any suspected fields destroyed immediately.

Naturally some cotton growers suffered by such actions, and there were often protests, ranging from disgruntled to violent, against the plan. At one point a rumor spread that bollworms were being deliberately planted as sabotage by agents of the Kaiser, and mob-mentality reprisals against the large German population of Texas were feared (but fortunately never actually happened).

And what effect did the bollworm's presence finally have? Well, not much, really. Pink bollworms did indeed become established throughout the Cotton Belt—they still are today—but their presence didn't change things to any great extent. They simply took their place on the ever-growing list of other agricultural pests and through efficient IPM programs are kept under control.

Both the boll weevil and the pink bollworm are still with us and no doubt always will be. Their entry into this country and their subsequent reluctance to leave make an important point in the story of human-insect relationships. Man may frequently proclaim himself to be the master of all creation, but it's clear that the insects of the world dispute that title.

CHAPTER EIGHTEEN

Deer

Zoologically speaking, a deer is any of certain artiodactyl ("even-hoofed") mammals, the mature males of which usually bear antlers that are shed and regenerated annually. Deer in various shapes and sizes are estimated to have been around for about thirty or forty thousand years. Today's assortment ranges from the huge Alaskan moose to the dog-sized pudu of the Andes.

In common American usage, the term is a bit more restrictive. Most of us, by "deer," mean mule deer and whitetails and not moose, elk, or caribou, which actually are, of course, deer. To muddy the waters even further, what we call a "moose" is called an "elk" in Europe, and our "elk," which is a variety of the Old World "red deer," should properly be called a "wapiti."

In addition to the three native deer of Texas—white-tailed deer, mule deer, and elk/wapiti—several introduced species flourish here as well. Axis deer from India, sika deer from China and Japan, and fallow deer from Europe have all proven themselves able to adapt and procreate in various parts of the state, and their descendants are still around. These latecomer Texas deer are worthy of a book themselves, but the discussion here will be confined to the two more common species.

Both of our Texas deer are hunted extensively during the open season. Deer hunting is looked upon by some people as an archaic exercise in cruelty, and I'm forced to admit that this is sometimes true. There have always been those humans who experience pleasure through inflicting pain and suffering on other creatures, and some of those humans use deer hunting as an excuse to do so. If there were some reasonable way to prevent this, I'd certainly do it. However, aside from having every hunter or every deer constantly accompanied by a personal game warden, it doesn't seem possible.

There are also people who say that hunting is an immoral act. There's really nothing I can say to argue this point. The criteria for what is or is not "immoral" are part of every individual's personal belief system. All of us have such a belief system, very few of them match exactly, and it's difficult if not impossible to change someone else's. I have no intention of trying to do that here.

Lastly we have those who believe that hunting is depleting wildlife populations and/or bringing about the extinction of game species. Unlike the first two opinion groups, there's no "gray area" here. Those people are simply flat-out wrong. Scientifically regulated hunting is not only not harmful to such species as white-tailed deer, it's actually helpful. Hard-hearted though it may sound, a deer's primary reason for existence is as a food source for carnivores. Because of this, they reproduce bountifully, ensuring that there will be enough individuals around to both fill the bellies of the meat-eaters and maintain the population. Should too few deer be killed by predators—wolves, pumas, or human hunters—the area becomes overpopulated. Resulting competition for available food will then both damage the environment and result in starvation of many of the "excess" deer anyway.

Although I've been fortunate enough never to suffer from near-starvation, I can easily imagine that it's quite the unpleasant experience. And I have seen deer in that situation—staggering dazedly through the snow, using their last vestiges of strength to try to reach the higher points on a tree trunk where other deer have not already stripped off the bark. From the perspective of physical comfort, I honestly believe I'd rather be walking through the autumnal forest, fat and happy, and be instantly killed by a rifle bullet.

Before I step down from this particular soapbox, I would like to conclude with a quote from biologist Robert L. Downing, possibly the world's foremost expert on American deer:

> No predator, insect, or disease has much effect on whitetail herds except at high deer densities.

Therefore the most practical management is to keep deer populations well below maximum density where they are individually healthy enough to resist most pests.

The most notable characteristic of deer is, of course, the antlers. This is one of the features that *make* them deer. In both white-tailed and mule deer, only mature males have antlers. (There are cases in which does have been found to grow antlers, but this is exceptional; it's the deer equivalent of a bearded lady. The caribou/reindeer branch of the family is the only one in which antlered females are normal.) It's commonly believed that the older the deer, the bigger the antlers, and vice versa, but this isn't quite true. Naturally a fully mature buck will sport a more impressive rack than will some wet-behind-the-ears adolescent, but antler size normally doesn't increase much after the age of four or five. Nutrition is the biggest determinant: Bucks that eat better grow bigger antlers, period. There may also be a genetic factor involved, but if so, it's probably of minor consequence.

Antlers grow from a skin-covered pedicel on the deer's head. In the early stages (late spring to summer) the antlers are a living part of the body, composed of a soft bony core and covered with a skin rich in blood vessels—the velvet, in common terms. If you ever have the experience of touching the velvety antlers of a live animal, you'll notice that they're unusually warm, a result of the rapid blood circulation.

By fall the buck's antlers have ceased to grow and are mostly hard bone. The now-dead velvet begins to slough off like the peeling skin following a bad sunburn. Either it itches uncomfortably, or there is some instinct that compels the deer to get rid of it. They constantly rub their antlers against any convenient surface until every scrap of velvet is removed. The antlers are often bloody at this time, but it's only the leftover fluids that died with the velvet, and not a result of self-injury.

Exactly what purpose do antlers serve? The obvious assumption is that they're defensive weapons, and this is correct to a point. Deer antlers have been directly responsible for the death of wolves, coyotes, bobcats, at least one black bear, and several humans—a laudable record of effectiveness. Yet the female has no antlers, and even the males have to do without them during most of the winter, when predators are hungriest. So, it would seem that this is not the main argument in their favor.

Many people, including myself, are of the opinion that antlers are primarily for dueling among rival bucks for the favors of the ladies. Despite the intensity of these quarrels, the participants are not usually injured to any extent. They can be, of course. A lucky (or unlucky, depending on which side you're on) blow with an antler can puncture an artery or put out an eye. And then there's the possibility that the two bucks will get their antlers permanently locked together. If this happens, not only will neither one get the girl, but they'll both starve to death.

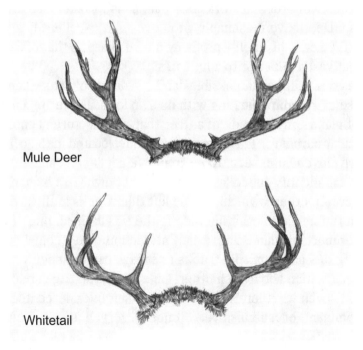

Mule Deer

Whitetail

After the fall rut—the mating season—the buck's antlers are shed. Dominant bucks—those who have gathered themselves a harem of responsive does—keep their antlers for some time longer than the bucks who didn't do as well. This is another point in favor of the argument that antlers are only for breeding season squabbles. Those who don't need them get rid of them earlier. In modern times, most shed antlers are collected by humans for a variety of reasons. Some of these castoffs are shipped to the Far East for their supposedly medicinal value. Others are carved into buttons, curios, and knife handles. Many become impressive chandeliers in ranch houses and hunting lodges. Those that escape human notice may be gnawed for their mineral content by mice, rabbits, porcupines, and even other deer.

Deer occasionally do battle with predators, but this is usually a last resort. For the most part, their defensive strategy is to discover where the predators are, and then make it a point to be elsewhere. In order to work, this plan calls for keen senses, of course. Deer have reasonably good eyesight, excellent hearing, and a fair sense of smell—probably not so sharp as that of a coyote, but vastly superior to a human's.

Besides sniffing out possible danger, a deer's olfactory senses are useful in communicating with its own kind. There are a number of glands on the body of a deer that manufacture scents for particular purposes. The interdigital glands, located in the center of each cloven hoof, seem to be an individual deer's "signature." A doe can identify and follow the trail of her own fawn by sniffing at it, even if other fawns have also left their tracks in the area.

On the inside of each hind leg is the tarsal gland, one of the most important glands for social interaction. The scent left by rubbing this gland on tree trunks or foliage can tell deer a lot of key information about each other—age, sex, breeding condition, possibly even whether the owner of the odor considered itself to be dominant or submissive. I once observed several bucks "reading" the tarsal rub left by another, which was a big powerful specimen. Those who were also big and powerful seemed to be outraged by it; those who were a little on the wimpy side turned tail and fled. I suppose the message left could be roughly translated as "You want a piece of me, Punk?"

The sudoriferous glands, located on the forehead, are well developed in the older, dominant bucks and seem to be most active during breeding season. Bucks mark tree trunks and branches by rubbing their heads against them and usually try to stretch as high as possible while doing this. I would suppose this is to make themselves seem bigger to any potential challengers. Other apparently somewhat less important scent glands can be found on the outside of the ankles and around the eyes.

Urine is another important marking substance. Bucks can determine a doe's sexual readiness by a whiff at the spot where nature called, and does are believed to be able to get an idea of the general health and condition of a buck by the smell of his urine. Like most females, the doe wants to endow her offspring with the best genes she can find, so she will tend to seek out a suitable sire through smelling his trail.

Should a deer happen across an older patch, where most of the urine has evaporated, the spot is often licked to get a better "look" at it. The vomeronasal gland, located on the roof of the mouth, is believed to be a built-in urinalysis unit for just such an occasion. Should a buck happen to detect a doe in a sexually receptive condition, he curls his lip up—a distinctive reactive gesture known as the Flehmen response.

The whitetail, *Odocoileus virginianus*, also known as the white-tailed deer or Virginia deer, is the commonest game animal throughout the nation. It ranges from the Arctic to the Equator, and is found in almost every state. There are several varieties of the species: local breeds that have gradually changed from the norm through adaptation to their particular environment but still remain *O. virginianus*. Since deer tend to be "homebodies" and will not generally leave their own neighborhood unless forced to do so, inbreeding often occurs, resulting in distinctive local characteristics. Although some of these subspecies, such as Florida's Key deer, are threatened, the whitetail as a whole is still extremely abundant.

Speaking of deer that hate to leave their home range, a few years back, several surplus whitetail bucks were live-trapped at the Aransas National Wildlife Refuge on the Gulf Coast and relocated in various other parts of the state. One of these, which had been released in the Panhandle region near the New Mexico border, showed up again in the same trap at Aransas the following year. Apparently he was clever enough to find his way back home, yet foolish enough to be trapped a second time. Or maybe he just enjoyed the trip so much he wanted to do it again. I haven't been able to find out if anybody tried to retransplant the homesick deer, but I doubt if it happened. You know, these days a buck doesn't go nearly as far as it used to.

Texas is virtually lousy with white-tailed deer. The overall population fluctuates, as with any wild animal, but in an average year there are over three and a half million of them throughout the state. Deer of all types have always been one of the preferred "eatin' critters" for both indigenous people and newly arrived colonists, and the whitetails of the Lone Star State provided many a meal for its human inhabitants. There was also a ready market for the leather. Between 1844 and 1853, a single trading post in Waco shipped over seventy-five thousand deer hides to New York.

The white-tailed deer is basically a woodland creature. It is long-bodied, slim-legged, and runs with a bounding gait designed for dodging trees and leaping over obstacles. The jumping ability of a whitetail is legendary, as can be readily confirmed by anyone who has ever tried to fence them out of a garden.

Whitetails are also noted for their ability to survive on just about any food available. Given a choice they prefer such delicacies as tender leaf buds, succulent clover, and apples, but will eat almost anything if these items aren't on the current menu. Their stomachs have been found to contain the remains of such things as cigar butts, shoe leather, eggshells, ball-point pens, handkerchiefs, grasshoppers, bones, even fish. It should be noted that these were not desperate animals faced with starvation, but prime specimens in proper foraging ground. Apparently, a whitetail's initial reaction to anything out of the ordinary is to try to eat it.

Despite these gustatory adventures, however, the whitetail is generally known for choosing the most nutritious items available for most of its diet. In agricultural areas, many deer will completely ignore their "natural" foods in favor of corn, soybeans, or alfalfa and even seem to be choosy about picking the best of the crop. Naturally, this doesn't exactly endear the species with the farmers. Prior to the introduction of game laws (1907 in Texas), a white-tailed deer was as likely to be shot for crop protection as for its venison and buckskin.

One bizarre bit of Texas whitetail lore concerns the sporadic appearance of "velvethorns." As mentioned, all buck deer go through an annual stage where their antlers are soft and covered in velvety skin. Occasionally, however, there will be a small percentage of male deer that maintain their antlers in this condition permanently. These velvethorns may occur in other parts of the country as well, but the only place I've ever seen or even heard about them is in the Llano area, around Enchanted Rock. Although technically male, velvethorns are small and androgynous-looking. They apparently never get the chance to breed. During the rut, both bucks and does, sometimes even older fawns, seem to develop an intolerance toward velvethorns and will chase them away on sight. If these unfortunate outcasts manage to survive past the autumn, their freakish, often mis-shapen antlers simply rot away.

What causes velvethorns, and why do they appear in quantity some years and not at all in others? Nobody seems to know for sure, but I've heard a number of theories, ranging from plausible to laughable. Velvethorns are possibly created by something in the water, the seasonal abundance of a certain food plant, radioactive fallout, the phase of the moon during their parents' copulation, overcrowding in the deer herds, pesticides, hormonal imbalance, an ancient Indian curse, young fawns having their testicles damaged, the wrath of God, depletion of the ozone layer, and lab experiments by Extraterrestrials. Pick one, or think up your own. As far as I know, all experimental attempts to create velvethorns under controlled conditions have been unsuccessful.

In the western half of Texas and on to the Pacific, we find the mule deer (*Odocoileus hemionus*). Unlike the whitetail, which generally prefers forested country, the "mulie" is a deer of the mountains and desert. The first scientifically documented specimen of mule deer was collected on the Lewis & Clark Expedition. These explorers commented on the large, mule-like ears of the animal, which gave it its common name.

One of the most noticeable behavioral differences between the mule deer and the whitetail is the way they run. A whitetail is accustomed to tearing through forests, leaping and bounding. Mulies, being children of the open country, have developed a particular gait known as "stotting"—a sort of pogo-stick stride in which they bounce over the terrain with all four feet leaving the ground simultaneously. Although this is the mule deer's normal mode of quick-stepping, when hard-pressed it will break into a gallop.

Mule deer also vary in appearance by the region they inhabit. (One type, the black-tailed deer of the Pacific Northwest, was formerly considered a separate animal altogether but is now classified as a subspecies of mule deer.) The biggest mule deer are generally found in the Rocky Mountains; the smallest in the Sonoran Desert. Available food is a factor in final size, of course. A fawn from the tiny desert race can grow almost as large as its mountaineer kinfolk if provided a better diet. Oddly, the nutritional intake of the pregnant mule deer doe seems to have little or no effect on the birth weight of her offspring. This is not the case with the whitetail, where underfed does tend to produce punier fawns.

The fawns are born with white-spotted coats. The background color on a baby mule deer is medium to dark brown, as opposed to the orange coat of a whitetail fawn. The spots fade around the age of three months, and the typical winter coat, dark gray, is acquired. During the spring, mule deer molt into a more reddish color. Some people who have only seen mule deer in photographs do not seem to be aware of this seasonal color change. Almost every picture of a mule deer ever published is of winter-coated specimens. This is probably because deer with antlers make for better photos, and any deer that has antlers will also be wearing a winter coat.

A buck becomes sexually mature at about twelve to eighteen months of age, but it generally doesn't do him much good for several more years. The older and more powerful males of the region tend to gather up all available females for themselves, and the skinny young upstarts of the season rarely get to breed. Does are also capable of reproduction at a year or so, and they, of course, do get the chance to prove it. A first-time birth is usually a single fawn; after that twins are the norm, with triplets not uncommon.

In many areas, only about a quarter of each spring's fawns are still around a year later. Much of the mule deer's range is pretty harsh country, and a variety of natural factors—food shortages, drought, severe winters—weed out the less hardy of the breed. Predators take a toll also. Young mule deer are sometimes taken by coyotes, wolves, cougars, both black and grizzly bears, perhaps even by eagles. Making it to your first birthday is no small accomplishment if you're a mule deer, even if the bigger bucks do keep you in a state of sexual frustration for a while longer.

Like most mammals, the mule deer is subject to drastic population cycles: the "Boom" years and the "Bust" years. The year 1998 seemed to be a "Bust" year, as mule deer numbers were at one of their lowest points in a decade. Unfortunately, there are signs that this may be something worse than the normal population fluctuation.

The biggest threat to the mule deer seems to be loss of habitat. The species' preferred type of country is broken, rocky scrub, and there just isn't nearly as much of that around as there used to be. The mountains of the West have, fairly recently, become one of the nation's hottest "status addresses." As a result, more chunks of mule deer range are being transformed into golf courses and landscaped mini-ranches every day. Those parts of the region that are maintained in the "wild" state are usually managed for the benefit of grasslands and timber—excellent elk habitat, but not suitable for mule deer.

Another problem, directly related to habitat alteration, is the westward expansion of the whitetail. As you know (especially if you read the first part of this chapter), the white-tailed deer is an opportunistic survivor, living anywhere it can, on anything it can find. As the mulie has retreated before the combined effects of reforestation and development, his eastern cousin has moved in. Whitetails are more than happy to skulk in the timber all day and come out for a nocturnal raid on a vegetable garden or topiary hedge. When they move in, they also directly compete with the remaining mule deer for whatever natural browse is still available.

Humans are responsible for the mule deer's decline, of course, but is there really anything we can do to stop it? Will the mule deer eventually follow in the path of the buffalo and become a semidomesticated curiosity, kept around for nostalgia's sake? Or will the pressures of natural selection transform it into a timber-dwelling, cornfield-raiding equivalent of the whitetail? Or will it disappear completely? I wish I knew the answers.

CHAPTER NINETEEN

Rattlesnakes

As mentioned in Chapter Eleven, a great many human beings have phobias—irrational fears—about a great many things, and one of the commonest of these concerns snakes. Spiders apparently repulse people due to having too many legs; I suppose snakes repulse people because they don't have enough. There are lots of folks in the world who are so scared of snakes that just the sight of one, even a totally harmless one, can literally paralyze them with fear. And there are even more folks who, while not quite that scared of snakes, would still just as soon not have them around.

In Judaeo-Christian tradition, the serpent is an evil creature. As a consequence of its role in getting Adam and Eve to eat the forbidden fruit, the snake was "cursed above all cattle and above every beast of the field." The physical manifestations of this curse consisted of confiscating the snake's legs: "... upon thy belly thou shalt go, and dust shalt thou eat all the days of thy life." Seems to me that that was ample punishment already, and that there's really no reason for us to continue persecuting the poor limbless creature.

Whether or not you choose to believe that God removed the serpent's legs personally, the fact remains that it used to have them. Study of the fossil record reveals that prehistoric snakes were basically lizards and scurried about on four legs like most lizards continue to do nowadays; and then they lost their legs. Even now there are a few "transitional" species around; some lizards don't have legs and some snakes (boas and pythons, for example) have "spurs" where their hind limbs used to be. In order to fit these middle-of-the-road species into the proper slot and figure out once and for all just who was a snake and who wasn't, zoologists came up with a checklist of three major features. Ears, eyelids, and legs are the deciding factors. If it has any two out of three, it's a lizard; otherwise it's a snake.

Some snakes are, of course, capable of killing people. Most rattlesnakes are among that category, hence rattlesnakes are dangerous. More correctly, rattlesnakes are potentially dangerous. They don't bite people out of cruelty or for the fun of it. Every rattlesnake bite I've ever heard of happened because the snake felt threatened somehow, and quite often the human "victim" deliberately initiated the contact. Of course, it's also quite possible to make a snake feel threatened without even being aware of its presence, and this can result in an innocent passerby being bitten. Caution should always be exercised whenever traveling in rattlesnake country: Watch where you step, watch where you sit down, and never ever stick your hand (or any other body part, for that matter) into a hole or crevice. If there happens to be a snake in there, the odds are pretty good that it's going to bite you.

Most cases of death by snakebite are, tragically, small children. Despite a common belief to the contrary, humans are not born with any "instinctive" repulsion towards snakes. Most toddlers see little difference between a coiled rattlesnake and a fuzzy baby duck and will often attempt to pick up and cuddle either one of these they happen to come across. And, of course, most wild snakes are unclear on the concept of cuddling. They think they're being attacked and will react accordingly.

In order to understand why snakes bite, try to put yourself in their situation: armless, legless, deaf, mute, and—to be bluntly honest about it—not particularly intelligent. The only way to get anything to eat is to hunt down some creature small enough to swallow whole, and the only way to hunt down anything is to slither along on your belly. While doing so—slithering along, that is—some other animal many times larger than you are lumbers into the scene and steps on you! Well, of course you'd bite the big oaf, wouldn't you? What other way would you have of expressing your displeasure at the situation?

All rattlesnakes belong to the group known as "pit vipers," so-called due to the presence of pits on its members. In case some readers are wondering how snakes can possibly have pits when they don't have any arms, a little clarification may be in order here. These are a different sort of pits. What they are, you see, are holes found on each side of the head, between and slightly below the eye and the nostril. Each pit actually consists of two cavities, an inner and an outer, separated by a thin membrane. Although exactly how the pits work is still a matter of some speculation, the fact that they do work, and very well, is an established fact. These are heat-sensing organs, able to distinguish temperature differentials as small as one degree from distances up to twelve feet. No warm-blooded creature (bird or mammal) can possibly hide from a pit viper, even in total darkness.

With the exception of the coral snakes, all venomous serpents found in North America are pit vipers—the cottonmouth (water moccasin), copperheads, and all species of rattlesnake. There are many other pit vipers throughout the world, some relatively well known and others fairly obscure. All are venomous, and all have triangular-shaped heads (with pits, of course). The South American bushmaster and the Gaboon viper of Africa are pit vipers. So are the fer-de-lance, jararaca, habu, Chinese mountain viper, white-lipped tree serpent, and others too numerous to mention. Rattlesnakes, however, are a distinctly American group.

It's generally believed that the original rattlesnake developed in central Mexico (a long, long time ago) and spread out from there. As with most other animals, there is some disagreement in scientific circles as to exactly which varieties of rattlesnake are distinct species and which are merely subspecies. For the purposes of this book, I'm going by the information provided in *A Field Guide to Western Reptiles and Amphibians*, by Robert Stebbins (see Bibliography), and say that there are eight species native to Texas, each of which this chapter will cover in some detail.

The rattle of a rattlesnake is composed of an interlocking series of hard, horn-like rings attached to the end of the tail. Although commonly believed that the number of rings in the rattle is equal to the number of years its owner has been alive, this isn't exactly true. As a general rule, snakes with more rings on their rattles are older. One more ring is added to the rattle every time the snake sheds its skin, which may be once a year and may not be, depending on conditions. Young, fast-growing rattlesnakes may add three or four rings to their rattles within a year's time. Rattles can also be broken off during the course of the snake's life, adding further confusion.

Snake venom is a veritable witch's brew of toxic substances, varying tremendously between species and even between individuals of the same type. Exactly why some snakes are equipped with this weaponry, and some are not, is something of a mystery. All snakes are predators, consequently it seems as though all would find venom to be quite useful in subduing their dinner. All snakes are also subject to being stepped on by larger animals, so it seems that all would benefit from some form of defense against this. The vast majority of the world's serpents, however, are neither venomous enough to hurt a human with their bite, nor big enough to kill one of us by constriction. In short, they're harmless. Most of them are also beneficial in keeping the rodent population under control, so they shouldn't be harmed. If you don't like snakes, that's certainly your business, but it doesn't convey the right to kill them on sight.

A rattlesnake's venom is stored in two sack-like organs in the head and can be injected through the fangs at will. It seems as though each snake can decide how much venom it wishes to use in any given situation and control the flow accordingly. The fangs themselves are merely sharpened hollow tubes and, without the sacks of venom to back them up, are basically harmless. Every now and then the stories go around about people dying because they accidentally touched an old rattlesnake fang imbedded in a boot or automobile tire. Some of these have become almost as popular as the one about the maniac's hook being found on the car door handle but have just about the same amount of truth in them (little to none). Regardless of how big the rattlesnake or how much effort it was putting out at the time it lost its fang(s), it's doubtful that enough venom could remain in the detached tooth to actually hurt anybody.

Anyone who has read this far into the book has probably gathered from my anecdotes that "self-employed naturalist" is not an overly lucrative profession. In order to finance my career, I've had to break down and get an actual job every now and then, but I'm always on the lookout for anything that will allow me to pick up a few extra dollars while wandering through the wilderness.

At the time of the following story, I was the caretaker on a remote chunk of West Texas acreage. The owner was a city dweller who wanted a place to go hunting in the fall, but had neither the time nor the desire to visit his property any more frequently than that. In exchange for room and board, I kept an eye on the place the rest of the year. Of course, I had to find other ways to obtain what little spending money I needed in those care-free days. I did day work on neighboring ranches, shod horses now and then, ran a small trap line in season, and sold fossils I collected to the local rock shops. None of these activities was ever going to make me rich, of course, so when I heard a rumor that one of the army units at Fort Bliss, Texas, was looking to buy live rattlesnakes, it sounded like a golden opportunity.

It took several days and a lot of phone calls to find anyone who actually knew what was going on with this matter. It took another day and a lot more phone calls before I found anybody who was actually authorized to discuss it. Finally, after one more day and another five or ten sessions with Ma Bell, I was put in touch with a Major Cox, whom I took to be the U.S. Army's resident Offi-cer-in-Charge-of-Procuring-Venomous-Reptiles. I arranged an appointment with the major at his office to receive the details of the assignment.

Major Cox, who looked an awful lot like Theodore Roosevelt, tested my credentials by seeing if I could correctly identify some pictures of various common snakes he had apparently cut out of a field guide. I guess I passed, because he offered me the job imme-diately. But I still sometimes wonder if anyone else had actually applied for it.

The gist of the situation was that Major Cox, or someone above him in the chain of command, had decided to assemble a rattlesnake collection for training purposes. Many of the soldiers stationed at Fort Bliss had apparently grown up in rattle-snake-free surroundings and needed to be taught to recognize them. (Although I had trouble believing, both then and now, that anybody could fail to recognize a snake with a rattle on its tail as being a rattlesnake, I kept that opinion to myself.). What the Army wanted from me was one healthy adult specimen of each species of rattlesnake indigenous to El Paso County, delivered within ninety days, for which I would be paid what seemed quite a princely sum to me at the time. Of course, I jumped on that offer like a duck on a June bug. The way I looked at it, if the govern-ment was going to waste the taxpayers' money, they might as well waste it on me. (I later found out that no governmental funds were actually involved. All the costs of the rattlesnake project had been raised by the soldiers and their families through such methods as bake sales and car washes. I had to admire that.)

In my youthful enthusiasm, I had signed an impressively legal-looking agreement before I had actually read every word of it (not an especially bright thing to do, as you may know). Although the written contract was basically the same as the ver-bal one set forth by Major Cox, it seemed that his idea of "indigenous to El Paso County" didn't completely agree with mine, as I found out later.

According to the contract, I was required to supply one each of the following: black-tailed rattlesnake (*Crotalus molossus*); rock rattlesnake (*C. lepidus*); prairie rattlesnake (*C. viridis*; western diamondback (*C. atrox*); and massasauga (*Sisturus catenatus*). So far, so good, but the list also included the Mojave rattlesnake (*Crotalus scutulatus*). Although I had heard of these, I'd never yet seen one; it was my belief that they weren't found locally. Major Cox was having none of this, however.

Brandishing a 1951 edition of an agricultural bulletin, which clearly showed the Mojave rattler's range map extending into El Paso County, the man would not be convinced otherwise. In as courteous a vocabulary as the subject matter would permit, Major Cox explained that the U.S. Army was more inclined to take the word of an official government publication than that of some unknown and wet-behind-the-ears cowboy who happened to drift in. And if the Department of Agriculture stated that there were Mojave rattlesnakes in El Paso County, well then, by God, that was good enough for him. Furthermore, if I wasn't capable of fulfilling my end of the bargain I shouldn't have agreed to it, and I was coming dangerously close to not only losing my present contract but being blacklisted for any future assignments.

I seriously doubted the idea of any "future assignments" ever materializing. Although the possibility did exist, it wasn't much of a concern to me. What raised my dander was the implication that I couldn't handle the task. My pride was at stake here. I decided that not only would I deliver the snakes as promised, *C. scutulatus* included, but then I'd tell that pompous major where he could stuff them (after I got paid, of course).

The black-tailed rattlesnake was no problem; I actually found one on the way back home from my first meeting with Major Cox. This is a relatively small snake, two to four feet long and is a relatively nonaggressive species as well. Of course, all rattlesnakes should always be treated with careful respect, small and nonagressive though they may be.

The black-tailed rattlesnake is partial to rocky areas. Although its overall coloration can vary from basically gray to basically yellow or olive-green, its sharply contrasting black tail usually makes identification simple (and also provided an easily remembered common name). The specimen I collected was average-sized, about a yard long, and seemed to be well fed and in good shape. I could only hope he stayed that way after "reporting for duty" with the military. My animosity was temporarily forgotten, and I made a note to supply written care and feeding instructions with the snakes when I delivered them.

I next acquired a western diamondback. These can grow up to seven feet long under ideal conditions. The one I captured was slightly over half that. Like all of his species, he was beautifully patterned, with dark hexagonal markings—"black diamonds" —on a tan background. The colloquial name of "coontail rattler" was evidenced by the arrangement of dark and light rings on the tail.

Due to their large size and irritable temperament, diamondbacks are extremely dangerous—probably the most dangerous snake in the state. Of course, like most potential hazards, common "wisdom" makes them out as even more dangerous than they actually are. Many people will be happy to tell you that this snake can strike faster than the eye can follow (nonsense; its strike is no faster than a trained boxer's left jab). The diamondback has also been credited with "hypnotizing" its prey, lying in wait for unwary humans to bite (apparently just for the fun of it), tracking down and seeking vengeance upon someone who killed its mate, and just about all of the other ridiculous things snakes are supposed to do, but don't.

There are two main varieties of the rock rattlesnake, the mottled (*C. lepidus lepidus*) and the banded (*C. l. klauberi*). Both can be found in West Texas, although the mottled seems to be more common here. Its banded kinfolk are primarily New Mexico and Arizona dwellers. The length of these is rarely more than a foot or two, and their pattern is distinctive. The gray background is marked with darker (brown to black) bands, wider at the top and narrow at the sides, regularly spaced down the length of the body. Rock rattlesnakes tend to be found in rocky areas, which is no great surprise. I couldn't find one in El Paso County, but I came across a foot-long specimen basking on the rocks of neighboring Hudspeth County.

Prairie rattlers are simply one variety of the western rattlesnake. This common species ranges just about everywhere west of the Mississippi, from southern Canada down into Mexico, and lives in a wide selection of habitats. Most of the subspecies have names indicating their home territory: Grand Canyon rattlesnake, Great Basin rattlesnake, Pacific rattlesnake, etc. The overall color of a western rattler seems to harmonize with the predominant color of the soil in its region. I've seen them in various shades of brown, cream, gray, green, yellow, and even pink. Rather than the clean-cut, well-defined diamonds or bands of many other rattlesnakes, the back pattern of *C. viridis* is somewhat blotchy. These irregular spots also vary in color but are always darker than the background. The one I collected for my assignment was sort of dark beige with brown highlights. Prairie rattlers can sometimes approach six feet in length, but three to four feet is the norm.

The massasauga is a relatively small snake, rarely exceeding three feet. It's usually darker in color than most other rattlers, sometimes almost black. There's a row of large, irregularly rounded spots down the back, three rows of smaller spots on the sides, and a set of elongated spots on the head and neck. The head alone can distinguish all members of the genus *Sistrurus* from its cousin in *Crotalus*. The former have several large "plates" in the area between the eyes, instead of many small scales. This is the "swamp rattler" of East Texas, a name bestowed upon it due to its preferred habitat. In the Trans-Pecos region, where swamps are few and far between, there is a sub-species known as the desert massasauga. This was, of course, the type I collected for the military's use.

All of the above were gathered together within two week's time. I had fashioned temporary living quarters for them out of empty fifty-five-gallon drums, half filled with clean soil and fitted with wire mesh lids. They seemed to have adjusted to captivity with no problems, and one of them even ate a mouse I provided. (Rattlesnakes don't eat all that often; a square meal will hold them anywhere from a week to a month or more.) Everything was going along splendidly, *except* for the Mojave rattlesnake.

I had researched *C. scutulatus* thoroughly. I knew that it was two to four feet long, usually light-colored, and had dark gray to brown hexagonal markings down its back. I knew that its tail was marked with alternating light and dark bands, that the scales on its snout were enlarged, and that it was an easily excitable spe-cies with a potent venom. In every reference I consulted, the range of the Mojave rattlesnake was listed as being from Nevada and Arizona to "extreme western Texas." Damn! Every expert said they were here; why couldn't I find one?

As my deadline drew near, I decided that I wouldn't give Major Cox the satisfaction of seeing me fail in my mission, even if I had to cheat a bit. I *bought* a Mojave rattlesnake from a reptile dealer in Arizona and delivered it along with those I had captured on my own. Unfortunately, the dealer's asking price for the snake was only a few dollars less than what I got paid for the entire collec-tion, but at least I had saved face with the Army.

A few months following the completion of Operation Rattle-snake, I was having a beer in an El Paso bar when I noticed a snakeskin band on the hat of one of the other patrons. Could it be...? Yes it was—a Mojave rattlesnake, unmistakably. I struck up a conversation with the man beneath the hat, who, it turned out, loved to talk. I soon knew all about the fellow: that he was a garage mechanic and lived in a nearby suburban neighborhood; that he had a son, a daughter, a collie, and an occasional flare-up of hemorrhoids. Eventually I steered the dialogue around to his hatband.

"It was a rattlesnake," he proudly exclaimed. "My wife found it in the backyard while she was weedin' the flower garden. She killed it with the hoe. I made this band from its skin; first time I ever tried doin' that kind of thing. Looks pretty nice, don't it?"

"Yup," I had to agree. "Looks pretty nice."

Other parts of the Lone Star State play host to other types of rattlesnake. One of the better known is *Crotalus horridus*. The subspecies *C. h. horridus* is generally known as the timber rattlesnake, while *C. l. atricaudatus* is called the canebrake rattlesnake. Both flavors can exceed six feet, and both have been known to give fatal bites.

The timber rattler, also known as the "banded" or "velvet-tailed" rattlesnake, is found from central Texas all the way to the Atlantic and is the only rattlesnake found in much of its range. A few years ago I saw a newspaper article about a den of hibernating rattlers being discovered in New York's Central Park. The story didn't identify the species, but I'm sure it was the timber type.

Winter denning is one of the timber rattlesnake's pronounced characteristics. It can sometimes be found in groups of several hundred, although this is becoming rare nowadays. Like many another creature that once existed in large groups, rattlesnakes have been affected by human activity in their territory and often find it prudent to form smaller congregations. If undisturbed, the snakes emerge in the spring and disperse throughout the countryside, then return to their communal den with the approach of cold weather.

Timber rattlesnakes come in two distinct color phases, the yellow and the black, which are pretty much self-explanatory. Both types have darker chevrons down the back, breaking up on the sides to form a row of spots down each "flank." The pattern may not be readily visible in the black phase but can be seen by anyone who wants to get close enough to look carefully (not often recommended).

The canebrake rattler is the more southern subspecies. It is also found from Texas on east but rarely strays north of Virginia. Although it does live in canebrakes, this isn't its only habitat; swamplands and wooded areas also have their share of these snakes.

The general appearance of a canebrake rattler is quite similar to that of a timber rattler. Coloration tends to be reddish-brown or even a little pink, but the pattern of bands is basically the same. The primary difference is the presence of a reddish stripe down the back, bisecting the chevrons.

As can easily be surmised, the pygmy rattlesnake *Sistrurus miliarius* is one of the smaller members of the family. The longest one for which I can find any reliable record measured a whopping twenty-five and one-eighth inches. The longest one I've personally seen was just under twenty inches. Like the closely related massasauga, the pygmy rattler has large plates on the crown of its head.

There are three recognized subspecies. *S. m. streckeri*, the western pygmy rattlesnake, is the only one indigenous to Texas. It's usually somewhat pale in color, gray to light brown, with a variable pattern of either spots or bars on the back. This little snake's rattle is so puny that it sounds more like the buzz of a horsefly than the warning signal of a venomous viper. Yet venomous it is, of course, like all rattlesnakes.

Most of the western half of Texas is too dry for the pygmy rattlesnake's tastes, so it's primarily found in the Piney Woods and

Gulf Coast areas. According to most literature on the topic, pygmy rattlesnakes are never found far from water. I suppose they could survive in the riparian areas of West Texas, but so far they haven't been able to cross the barren deserts to get to them.

"Rattlesnake Roundups" are a common event in Texas and in several other states as well. I don't see anything wrong with the basic idea of these gatherings: spend a few days wandering through the local outback, collect a few rattlesnakes, display them to the public. When the show's over, process the snakes for their meat and hides—a natural use of a natural resource.

Unfortunately, many (not all, by any means, and probably not even most) snake hunters and snake handlers twist the pastime into something both ecologically unsound and morally questionable. Harvesting rattlesnakes the old-fashioned way, by happening to come across them, is not likely to have any detrimental effect on the wild population. Rattlesnakes try to avoid humans whenever possible (and most of them are pretty good at it), so for every one that's found there are plenty more that aren't.

The problem is that, for any number of reasons—time constraints, laziness, the ego factor at getting a big catch—some unscrupulous snake hunters go around spraying gasoline or other volatile chemicals down "snake holes" to try to flush out their quarry. Besides poisoning parts of the planet in general, which most of us agree is a bad thing to do, this practice results in the death or injury of anything else that may be in those holes. Insects, spiders, spadefoot toads, burrowing owls, black-footed ferrets, or whatever is in there are going to suffer as a result. As a general rule, whatever creatures inhabit the wilderness, be they microbes or elephants, are there because they're supposed to be there. Indiscriminately wiping out an entire microenvironment, even if it's just a hole in the ground, can easily result in long-range disaster to the macroenvironment of which it was a part. Introducing a congressional bill to have people who spray gasoline down holes in the ground publicly horse-whipped wouldn't bother me at all.

Even if the snakes were obtained through legitimate methods, their fate in captivity is sometimes a cruel one. I have nothing against putting animals on display; it's the only chance much of the public ever has to see them. I do have something against inhumane treatment of the specimens, which rattlesnakes frequently seem to receive. There is absolutely no justifiable reason for the captive snakes to be constantly prodded and tormented, kicked around in their enclosures, or beaten with sticks; but it often happens.

Attend just about any rattlesnake roundup these days and you will usually find a few protesters outside the entrance. Occasionally these picketers are part of the same type of lunatic fringe that tries to break into snail farms to free the breeding stock, or plants firebombs in laboratories that use white rats for cancer research. For the most part, though, the people who protest the roundups are sane, well-meaning folks who are simply opposed to wanton cruelty. I can see their side of it, although I disagree that the event itself is the problem. It's the attitude of some of the participants that needs fixing.

CHAPTER TWENTY

The Armadillo

I began this book with a chapter on the Texas long-horn—the animal that once was the very symbol of Texas itself. Now, as the twentieth century draws to a close, another species has come to be regarded as the totemic creature of the Lone Star State. This is, of course, the armadillo.

The armadillo craze has died down a bit nowadays. At the peak of its frenzy, the critter was turning up everywhere. There were armadillo-themed belt buckles, bolo ties, Christmas ornaments, and cookie cutters. Cartoon armadillos advertised everything from beer to pickup trucks. The mania even reached the Far East. I came across the "Armadillo Cabaret," complete with a neon representation of the animal flashing above the doorway, in the heart of Tokyo's nightclub district. (I didn't go in, though; the cover charge was too steep.)

Our local Texas armadillo is the nine-banded *Dasypus novemcinctus*. It's merely one member of a varied family of other armadillos found from Mexico south to Patagonia. Besides the familiar nine-banded, there are also three-banded, six-banded, and seven-banded varieties. In addition, there are hairy armadillos and naked-tailed armadillos. There's a northern long-nosed armadillo and a southern long-nosed armadillo. There's a giant armadillo, which can weigh over a hundred pounds, and there's the pink fairy armadillo, which is barely the size of a hamster. (I personally prefer to call this last species by its local Argentine name of *pichiciego*; "pink fairy" sounds like fightin' words where I come from.)

The nine-banded armadillo's high profile (in the cultural sense, that is; not its physical size) has earned it a number of affectionate nicknames. Many of these refer to its edibility: During the Great Depression, when many citizens were first driven to eating wild game, the armadillo was known as the Hoover hog.

Today it is often referred to as Texas turkey or possum on the half shell. Armadillo barbecues are fairly common events. There are even cookbooks devoted entirely to armadillo recipes, although most of these are probably bought as gag gifts, by Texans, for non-Texans.

Armadillos are biologically classified as edentates, meaning toothless animals, but this is erroneous. Armadillos do have teeth: Our nine-banded species has about thirty of them, and the giant armadillo can have over a hundred. They aren't very impressive teeth, as teeth go; they're small and peg-like, with a single root and an open pulp cavity. These teeth aren't capable of inflicting any sort of bite damage. About all they're good for is mashing up insects. Coincidentally enough, that's just what the armadillo uses them for.

Insects, worms, and other small invertebrates make up most of the armadillo's diet. Some plant matter is also eaten, and so is a lot of dirt. Because they dig for most of their food and basically slurp it up whole when they find it, armadillos can't help ingesting quite a bit of the surrounding countryside. The animal's droppings are sometimes as much as seventy-five percent soil. Although the dirt is most likely eaten unintentionally, it may supply some needed minerals in the armadillo's diet.

The digging habit hasn't exactly endeared armadillos with greenskeepers on the golf courses of Texas, nor with suburbanites who like well-manicured lawns. It has also led to a widespread belief that armadillos eat corpses, due to the fact that they seem drawn to fresh graves. I seriously doubt that any armadillo has ever developed a taste for human flesh, dead and buried or otherwise. For one thing, they wouldn't be able to chew it with those wimpy little teeth of theirs. I think fresh graves attract them for the same reason that any other recently turned earth does; it's easier to dig in. Nobody has ever accused armadillos of being incredibly intelligent, but I think they're probably bright enough to grasp that concept.

The fairly recent spread of the nine-banded armadillo is something of a mystery. Many zoology books from the turn of the century contain statements such as "armadillos occasionally wander across the Rio Grande into extreme south Texas." They can now be found not only over most of Texas, but also in Oklahoma, Arkansas, Louisiana, Mississippi, Alabama, Georgia, and Florida, plus there have been unverified sightings in other states. Of course, human activity is responsible for part of the dispersion. Armadillos transported to other areas for novelty pets, or for later use as a pot of stew, no doubt escaped from captivity every now and then. But for the most part the critter has expanded its territory on its own, boldly pioneering new habitats, and the only real barrier seems to be cold weather. The armadillo doesn't have enough hair on its body to withstand a severe winter, and so far it hasn't learned how to hibernate. I seriously doubt that armadillos will ever colonize Alaska or New England, even if they managed to spread that far during the warmer parts of the year. Of course, with the current trend towards global warming, it may happen yet.

Personally, it seems to me that armadillos have been crossing the Rio Grande into Texas much more often than "occasionally" for quite some time—probably since 1850 or so. In 1879 an armadillo, reported to have been captured nearby, was displayed in San Antonio as a curiosity. Within a decade, they were showing up in the butcher shops. By 1930 armadillos were so common in South Texas they were being shot as vermin.

Armadillo hunting could hardly be classed as a hazardous sport, yet there may be some risk associated with it, provided the hunter eats his quarry. Armadillos, like humans, are capable of hosting a microbe known as *Mycobacterium leprae*, and *M. leprae* can infect its host with Hansen's disease—commonly known as leprosy.

The chances of contracting leprosy from an armadillo are probably pretty slim. As far as my research into the subject could discover, there have only been five known cases of it happening. (This doesn't mean there aren't a lot more that I didn't hear about, of course.) Apparently, thorough cooking of the meat destroys the bacilli responsible for transmission of the disease, so it's a good idea to serve your barbecued armadillo well done instead of medium rare (and never, ever, order armadillo sushi). Those unfortunates who were infected by armadillos seem to have contracted it through cuts or scratches received by handling the live animals and not by eating the cooked ones.

Small though the risk may be, it's still something to take seriously. Lately I've tried to form the habit of wearing gloves when handling wild animals. After all, it seems that one can catch leprosy from armadillos, hantavirus from mice, even bubonic plague from jackrabbits. None of these strike me as anything I'd really like to have, so I think it's only prudent to take precautions. I realize that I'm going to have to die eventually, but I'd just as soon put it off for a while longer.

Humans aren't the only creatures to develop a taste for armadillo, of course. Coyotes, bobcats, black bears, golden eagles, and mountain lions have all been known to feed on them in Texas, and domestic dogs will sometimes kill and eat an armadillo as well. (Foxes and raccoons might prey on young individuals once in a while, but I doubt they could handle a fully grown one.) Armadillo remains have been found in the stomachs of alligators, and I was told by a usually reliable witness that at least one large snapping turtle has killed and eaten an armadillo.

The little animal's "armor" isn't really a whole lot of protection against predators. It's commonly believed in some places that armadillos can roll themselves up into an impervious ball (yes, I've personally heard people say this), but it just ain't so. An armadillo's shell affords about as much protection as a cowboy's leather leggings: in other words, better than nothing. Both of these may help stave off cactus needles and mesquite thorns, but they aren't guaranteed against fangs and talons.

Armadillos have several survival strategies when attacked. The strong claws on their front feet are quite capable of inflicting injury on the enemy, but this is strictly a last resort. The primary plan is to try to get away. Armadillos aren't exactly in the same speed league as roadrunners or pronghorns, but they can run reasonably fast when the need arises. If they have a burrow nearby, they head for it in time of danger. Otherwise they may try to hole up in the brush or dig a new burrow on the spot.

An alarmed armadillo often jumps straight up in the air—sometimes more than once—before it makes a break for it. Possibly this tactic has some value against natural predators. Maybe it confuses them or makes it harder to line up a vital spot for the attack. Unfortunately, armadillos as a group haven't yet figured out that the jumping technique is useless against oncoming automobiles. This is the reason for another one of the species' common nicknames: Texas speed bump.

Armadillos are frequently used in medical research. In addition to their value as test animals for leprosy treatment, the armadillo's unusual reproductive system makes it a convenient subject for experiments in heredity and genetics.

Armadillo mothers always bear identical quadruplets. A single fertilized egg invariably divides into four embryos, either all males or all females. Genetically identical siblings make excellent study specimens for testing just about anything—vaccines, antibiotics, possible carcinogens, etc.—because it takes a lot of the individual variation out of the resulting reactions. The use of armadillos as a resource for advancing medical knowledge, and subsequently human health care, is a justifiable practice. I sincerely hope that armadillos (or any other life form, for that matter) are no longer used for testing nonessential products such as cosmetics. That to me is *not* justifiable.

Despite their apparent qualifications for the position, however, it doesn't look as though armadillos are ever going to replace white mice and guinea pigs in the world's research laboratories. For some as yet unknown reason, the nine-banded armadillo is extremely reluctant to reproduce in captivity. Many people have been trying for many years to breed armadillos with little or no success. Relying on wild-caught specimens for research seriously hampers the controlled conditions necessary for many experiments, so armadillos can't be used nearly as often as some scientists would like.

The entire sex life of the armadillo is still a relative mystery. Despite the fact that zoologists have seemingly replicated every possible aspect of the natural habitat for captive armadillos, they still won't breed regularly. Research facilities have bred captive cheetahs, orangutans, gorillas, and rhinoceroses, but they can't seem to breed armadillos. Why? Nobody seems to know yet.

Early attempts at "domestication" of the armadillo were hampered by the similarity in appearance of the sexes. (The same problem existed with whooping cranes, as recounted in Chapter Sixteen.) The male armadillo has no scrotum; his testicles are internal, as is the case with birds and reptiles. When captive armadillos failed to show any romantic interest in each other, it was often assumed that they were the same sex.

There are, however, a few cases of captive armadillos supposedly breeding. Maybe they did, maybe they didn't. The mothers in question may well have been "sort of pregnant" when captured. The female of the species is capable of storing the sperm from a romantic encounter inside her body for up to twenty months before actually fertilizing an egg with it. Naturally, this can make it somewhat difficult to pinpoint exactly when the magic moment took place (or, for that matter, the identity of the other party involved; armadillos tend to be promiscuous and do not seem to form long-term pair bonds).

For many years, armadillo curios were popular Texas souvenirs. The usual choice was a basket made from the cured shell, with the tail stuffed into the mouth to form a handle. Whether or not he actually invented this item is questionable, but the man who made it famous was Charles Apelt (1862-1944). Apelt had been a basket maker in his native Germany, and after moving to Texas in 1887 he saw the common armadillo from a fresh perspective. At its peak, the Apelt Armadillo Company (Comfort, Texas) was shipping out thousands of the baskets all over the world, as well as doing a brisk business in armadillo lampshades, armadillo chandeliers, whole mounted armadillos, and live specimens. Many of the nearby residents supplemented their incomes by catching armadillos for the firm. Interestingly, there were sometimes human casualties as a result. In their eagerness to capture armadillos for the price on their shells, overzealous hunters would sometimes reach into likely looking burrows to try and grab one. If you read Chapter Nineteen, you can guess where this is going. Not every hole in the ground is an armadillo hole.

Apelt's company suspended operations in 1971, but armadillo baskets are still something of a cottage industry in parts of Texas and Mexico. Not every basket is as well crafted as the ones Apelt turned out. His secret and well-guarded "scientific formula" of shell preservation guaranteed his products to be insect-proof and odor-free; other manufacturers can't always offer the same warranty.

For the most part, the bottom has dropped out of the shell basket market, so hunting pressure on the armadillo population has subsided along with it. Although still occasionally harvested for food, captured for pets (the popularity of this has also waned, however), or destroyed as a nuisance to golf courses, armadillos as a whole are not heavily persecuted. It was once widely believed that (in addition to robbing human graves) armadillos destroyed game bird nests. It seems as though every time there's a real or imagined dip in the population of quail, pheasant, or wild turkey, some other animal gets blamed for it. The armadillo had its own turn in this barrel, just as did the roadrunner (see Chapter Five). In 1933 Texas game warden Frank Smith was tasked with investigating the matter, and he absolved the armadillo of all guilt. Smith planted artificial "nests," stocked with chicken eggs, at strategic locations and kept an eye on who came a-callin'. The local coyotes, foxes, raccoons, possums, and skunks all took full advantage of the situation. Some of the nests were destroyed when stepped on by cattle. Armadillos, however, were not a factor. In his written report to the Texas Game, Fish, and Oyster Commission, Smith stated, "I want to see my little friend the armadillo's skirts cleared of this crime that is being heaped on his back by a lot of circumstantial evidence and the talk of a lot of town dudes who do not know an armadillo from a dry-land terrapin."

The armadillo's expansion is probably far from over. Not a year goes by without a few new armadillo sightings in previously unoccupied territory. (Of course, some of the same people who spot armadillos also spot UFO's, Bigfoot, and Elvis, so not every claim can be verified.) Reasonably reliable reports have come in from Kansas, New Mexico, Tennessee, South Carolina, and Colorado, sometimes with physical evidence to back them up.

Besides its low tolerance for cold weather, the other major stumbling block for the pioneering armadillos is aridity. Although some armadillo species are true desert animals, the nine-banded is not. It can't survive without a fairly regular supply of drinking water. Its westward migration is therefore limited to riparian environments. Will this put a halt to the continued spread of the armadillo? Only time will tell.

APPENDIX A

Classification of Animals

Until fairly recently, all living things were placed into one of two kingdoms—the Animal Kingdom and the Plant (or Vegetable) Kingdom. There were a number of microscopic life-forms that seemed to maintain dual citizenship in both of these, and those scientists who make it their business to classify things would often get into fistfights as to where these little blobs of protoplasm truly belonged. The field of biology was eventually overhauled to create a total of five kingdoms of living things, and there may even be a few more still waiting in the wings. As it currently stands (in most references), we have the kingdoms of *Monera* (bacteria and viruses), *Protista* (the amoebae and such critters), *Fungi* (mushrooms and mildew), *Plantae*, and *Animalia*. Fortunately, all twenty of my chapter subjects are still loyal subjects of the Animal Kingdom, so there's no need to discuss the others any further. (The biology section of any decent public library should have this information, should any readers want to learn more about it.)

After the Kingdom, which includes every animal from myself on down to the latest worm on my fishhook and the bass I hope to catch with it, there are a plethora of other headings. The basic ones (in descending order) are called Phylum, Group, Class,

Order, Family, Genus, and Species. Sometimes two or more of these are grouped together into a Superphylum, Superclass, etc., and they may be further divided into Suborders, Subspecies, and so on. With all this from which to select, biologists are continually creating new Subs and Supers and shooting down those created by their rivals. Individual animals are also sometimes shuffled between groups. The science of classifying life, like life itself, is continually on the move. No matter what sort of classification system I happen to use here, you can always find another book that disagrees with me. So when you do, don't bother to write and tell me; I already know.

The basic system is called "binomial nomenclature," which identifies every particular creature by its Genus and Species. I, for example—and you as well, I would assume—happen to be a *Homo sapiens*. My entire scientific pedigree would read like this:

Kingdom: *Animalia*: Animals.

Phylum: *Chordata*: Animals with a spinal cord.

Subphylum: *Vertebrata*: The spinal cord is contained within a backbone.

Class: *Mammalia*: The female nurses her young with milk produced in mammary glands.

Order: *Primates*: Well-developed cerebral structures and opposable thumbs.

Family: *Hominidae*: Humanoid-type creatures.

Genus: *Homo*: Humans.

Species: *sapiens*: Humans who are capable of logical thought (although this capability doesn't always seem to be used to its full advantage). I suppose I could, like the longhorn, be further broken down into the subspecies *texanus* if you wanted to go that far.

In the following pages, I will attempt to pigeonhole each of the main characters of this book into their proper slots. Since many of these terms are also common English words ("family," for example) I've capitalized them whenever used in the technical sense. This isn't actually correct for literary purposes, but I think it will make the text less confusing and easier to read. In general usage, when identifying an animal by its scientific name, the Genus is capitalized, while Species and Subspecies are not: hence, *Homo sapiens texanus*. When different Species of the same Genus are being discussed together, it's a common practice to abbreviate. For example, I might introduce a topic with the domestic dog, *Canis familiaris*, and later refer to the related coyote as *C. latrans*. Saves a lot of space on the page and wear on the keyboard! To beat that same drum one more time: Not everybody agrees with the system I'm using here.

Mammals

The Texas longhorn, ringtail, coyote, kangaroo rat, pronghorn, bat, javelina, deer, and armadillo are all mammals. As such, they belong to the same Class that I do, and we share a common lineage going upwards from that level.

Longhorns, pronghorns, javelina, and deer are all members of the Order *Artiodactyla*, meaning they have hooves with an even number of toes. One of the Families in this Order is *Bovidae*, which includes antelope, bison, buffalo, goat, sheep, and all breeds of cattle, which make up the Genus *Bos*. "Domestic" cattle are *Bos taurus*; the Texas longhorn is the Subspecies *Bos taurus texanus*.

The Family *Cervidae* is the deer. The Genus *Odocoileus* includes two Species: the mule deer *O. hemionus* and the whitetail *O. virginianus*. There are a number of Subspecies of each, with different schools of thought lumping these together or splitting them apart on the basis of various details.

The pronghorn, unique beast that it is, is the only Species in the only Genus in its Family. It is *Antilocapra americana*, from the family *Antilocapridae*. Over ninety percent of the pronghorns in the country belong to the main Subspecies *A. americana americana*. Some of our Texas stock is supposedly *A. americana mexicana* as well, but with frequent inbreeding of the two, the distinctions are not always clear.

Tayassuidae is the Family of peccaries. Both the white-lipped peccary and our native collared peccary, the javelina, are members of the Genus *Tayassu*. The javelina is *T. tajacu*.

The next Order on our agenda is the one called *Carnivora*. Its members, consequently, are known as *Carnivores*: eaters of meat. Scientifically speaking, not everything that eats meat, and is therefore a carnivore, is an actual *Carnivore*. I enjoy a good pork chop or T-bone steak myself, yet I've been a *Primate* all my life.

For classification purposes, the *Carnivores* are such things as bears, dogs, cats, weasels, hyenas, mongooses, and procyanids. Many, if not most, of these animals eat vegetable matter in addition to the flesh of their neighboring species. Bears, for example, eat an awful lot of nuts and berries and such. But *Carnivores* they are, regardless of such habits.

The Family *Canidae* is, of course, the dogs. Everything from French poodles to red foxes is covered here. Genus *Canis* is where we find the most dog-like of the dogs: *C. familiaris* (dogs), *C. lupus* (gray wolf), several lesser-known Species such as jackals, and our old friend the coyote *C. latrans*.

Remember the ringtail's kinfolks, the Family *Procyonidae*? One of its Genera (the plural of Genus, just in case you didn't already know that) is *Bassariscus*, and one of the two Species —the one found in Texas—is *B. astutus*.

All types of bats belong to the incredibly huge and diverse Order *Chiroptera*: the "wing-handed" animals. Due to its size, it's convenient to split this horde of bats into two Suborders, the

Megachiroptera and the *Microchiroptera*. Did any readers already figure out that this translates as big bats and small bats? Absolutely correct, but, unfortunately, also misleading. Some of the *Microchiroptera* are actually bigger than most of the *Megachiroptera*. Don't look at me, I didn't come up with this system!

Our Texas bats, in fact all American bats, are *Microchiroptera*. The free-tailed bats belong to the Family *Molossidae*, named for the "mastiff-headed" bats of the bunch. This Family is broken down into eleven Genera. The Genus with which we are here concerned is further divided into five Subgenera, which contain a total of fifty Species (at last count!). *Tadarida brasiliensis* is placed in the Subgenus *Tadarida*, which is the same name as its Genus (how convenient).

The pallid bat comes to us from the Family *Vespertilionidae*. Like most bat Families, it's a big one—thirty-seven Genera and over three hundred Species. The Genus *Antrozorus* is commonly known as desert bats. The pallid bat is *A. pallidus*.

American leaf-nosed bats comprise the Family *Phyllostomidae*. This is a medium-sized group by bat standards—a hundred and forty Species—belonging to forty-five separate Genera. The Mexican long-tongued bat, *Choeronycterus mexicana*, is the only Species in its particular Genus.

The ghost-faced bat comes from a rather small Family (which is actually quite understandable, considering the face on it—even motherly love can only go so far). There are two Genera in Family *Mormoopidae*, and two Species in Genus *Mormoops*, one of which is *M. megalophylla*.

And then there are the vampire bats, Family *Desmodontidae*. Although various other groupings of bats have titles that sound more like something Buffy would try to slay—*Vampyressa*, *Vampyrodes*, *Vampyrum*, etc.—these were largely given out in error. By the time the actual vampire bats were identified, all the sinister names were already taken. *Desmodontidae* is divided into three Genera, each of which contains but a single Species. The hairy-legged vampire is *Diphylla ecaudata*.

The Order *Rodentia* is, quite naturally, the rodents. This is another pretty sizable bunch and includes such things as beavers, porcupines, squirrels, mice, gophers—all those little buck-toothed critters that are constantly gnawing on things. The kangaroo rats are among them—Family *Heteromyidae*, Genus *Dipodomys*.

Armadillos of all shapes and sizes belong to the Family *Dasypodidae* of the Order *Edentata*. As mentioned in Chapter Twenty, the members of this Order are supposed to be toothless, but they forgot to tell the armadillo that, so it has teeth anyway.

Birds

Kingdom *Animalia*, Phylum *Chordata*, Subphylum *Vertebrata*, Class *Aves*: the birds. All birds are warm-blooded creatures with feathers, and they all lay eggs. Most of them can also fly, but this isn't a strict criterion for Class membership. Ostriches, kiwis, and penguins are birds, yet none of them can fly a lick.

The first Order pertinent to our discussion is *Falconiformes*. Falcons belong to this group, quite naturally, as do other types of hawks. Eagles and the African secretary bird are also members in good standing.

Accipitridae is the hawk and eagle Family. The Genus *Buteo* of this Family includes such hawks as the zone-tailed (*B. albonotatus*), white-tailed (*B. albicaudatus*), and gray (*B. nitidus*). The closely related Genus *Parabuteo* is where my personal hawk, the Harris' (*P. unicinctus*), calls home.

Last but most certainly not least we come to the Family *Falconidae*. This is represented in North America by eight Species in the Genus *Falco* (including the aplomado falcon, *F.*

femoralis) and one in the Genus *Polyborus—P. cheriway*, the crested caracara.

Until quite recently, the Family *Cathartidae* was considered a part of *Falconiformes* but is now generally placed into the *Ciconiidae* with storks and ibises. *Cathartidae* is divided into five Genera, including *Cathartes* (the turkey vulture is *Cathartes aura*) and *Coragyps* (*Coragyps atratus*, the black vulture).

In the Order *Gruiformes* we can find such exotic avian creatures as the roatelos, sun grebes, and kagu. We also find the Family *Gruidae*, the cranes, and within that the Genus *Grus*, one of which is our reknowned whooping crane, *G. americana*.

Cuculiformes is a diverse and widespread Order. One of its three Families is *Cuculidae*, and one of six Subfamilies under this heading is *Neomorphinae*. This Subfamily gives rise to six Genera, including *Geococcyx*, and *G. californianus* is the roadrunner.

Over a third of all living bird Families and more than half the total of all known Species belong to the Order *Passeriformes*. These are the familiar "perching birds," those with feet adapted for clinging onto tree branches (although these feet have been proven to work equally well on such things as fence wire and telephone lines, once mankind provided them for the birds' use). The numerous Families within *Passeriformes* are the domain of our common songbirds—robins, wrens, thrushes, etc.—as well as lyrebirds, birds of paradise, drongos, and many more. The northern mockingbird is Family *Mimidae*, Genus *Mimus*, Species *polyglottus*.

Reptiles

Reptiles have backbones, consequently *Reptilia* is another Class of *Vertebrata*. Three of the still-existing Orders in this Class are reasonably well defined: one for turtles, one for crocodilians, and one for the tuatara (a New Zealand reptile which looks a lot like a big lizard, but actually isn't one). After that it gets more complicated. If you read Chapter Nineteen, you may recall that the dividing line between snakes and lizards is sometimes a bit fuzzy. Depending on which reference one consults, there are various ways of classifying the two. Some prefer the Superorder *Squamata*, which contains the Order *Serpentes* for snakes and the Order *Sauria* for lizards. Others are partial to calling *Squamata* the Order and splitting up the snakes and lizards as Suborders or Superfamilies. I'm not taking any sides on this one.

Anyhow, this book has represented the Order/Suborder/ Superfamily *Sauria* with Genus *Phrynosoma* of the Family *Iguanidae*. These are our three native horned toads, *P. cornutum*, *P. modestum*, and *P. douglassi*. They may not look like most people's idea of iguanas, and yet iguanas they actually are—highly modified ones, of course.

All of our rattlesnakes are scions of the Family *Crotalidae* of the (insert group title of your choice) *Serpentes*. The massasauga and the pygmy rattlesnake belong to Genus *Sistrurus*, the others to Genus *Crotalus*. I could list all the Species here again, but it's already been covered quite thoroughly in Chapter Nineteen.

Fish

We'll wrap up *Vertebrata* with Class *Pisces*, the fish. Much like the classification of reptiles, the classification of fish is a veritable can of worms. Nobody seems to agree on much of anything. There are many biologists who feel that the entire Class *Pisces* should be scrapped and replaced with several more specialized ones. Even those who agree to keep old *Pisces* in the game want to break it into Subclasses, Subsubclasses, even Subsubsubclasses. I'm not going to mess with all of that in a book of this general nature. We'll let our alligator gar's family tree get by with Class *Pisces*, Subclass *Actinopterygii* (ray-finned fishes), Order *Semionotiformes* (gars), Genus *Atractosteus* (two rows of teeth in the upper jaw), Species *spatula*. In some versions *Semionotiformes* is replaced by *Lepisosteiformes*, but it still means gars.

Arthropods

Scorpions, vinegaroons, solpugids, spiders, and insects all belong to the Phylum *Arthropoda*, which also includes such things as shrimp, lobsters, and centipedes.

Class *Arachnida* contains both the spiders and the scorpion-like creatures. All true spiders, including tarantulas, are members of order *Araneae*. There are three main Suborders; tarantulas belong to the one known as *Orthognatha*. Our desert tarantula is Genus *Aphonopelma*, Species *chalcodes*.

Scorpion classification is currently undergoing even more revision than that of other living creatures. New species are constantly being discovered (thanks largely to the black light), and many of these show characteristics that call for the creation of new titles for the higher headings on the family tree. As of my latest delve into this field, the Texas bark scorpion was Order *Scorpionida*, Family *Buthidae*, Genus *Centruroides*, Species *vittatus*.

Vinegaroons are in Order *Amblypygi*; sunspiders in Class *Solifugae*. The respective Genus and Species are *Mastigoproctus giganteus* and *Eremobates pallipes*.

The Class *Insecta* (often now referred to as a Subclass of *Hexapoda*) is, of course, the insects. Due to the incredible number of insect species—millions of them known, with new ones being discovered almost daily—and the amount of diversification among them, there are more Subgroups and Supergroups involved than most readers would care to hear about. Beetles, including weevils, are members of the Order *Coleoptera*. To paraphrase Charles Darwin, the Lord must really love beetles, or He wouldn't have made so many of them. The pink bollworm is a moth in its adult life, so it falls into the Order *Lepidoptera* with all the other moths and butterflies. Tarantula hawks are classified in the Order *Hymenoptera*, which includes ants and bees as well as wasps.

APPENDIX B

Resources

Where to See Texas Wildlife

The ideal way to observe wildlife, of course, is in its natural habitat. Unfortunately, many people are too short on time/money to travel to the proper areas, or too short on outdoor skills to get close enough to wild animals to make the viewing worthwhile. If you happen to fall into one or both of these classifications, you can still see a lot of native Texas wildlife by visiting a zoo.

Just about every city of any size has a zoo these days, and most of them are excellently managed. Zoos in general have come a long way from the old days of pitiful animals crammed into steel cages and fed on garbage. (There are still a few places like that around, unfortunately, but at least they're on the decline.) The modern zoological garden is built and operated for the welfare of the animals—both the individuals in captivity and the various species as a whole—at least as much as for the entertainment of the public.

One of the better exhibits of native Texas species was found in the Victoria Zoo. I say "was" because, I'm sorry to report, it suffered considerable flood damage in 1998. On October 20 torrential rains caused the Guadalupe River near Victoria to crest at a level three feet higher than any previous record. Water reached six feet deep throughout the zoo, resulting in millions of dollars of damage to buildings, equipment, research materials, and even caused the loss of some of the animals. This was a terrible tragedy for both the zoo itself and for the public.

For those who wish to see free-roaming animals, Texas has a whole slew of parks and wilderness areas where this can happen. There are a number of excellent guidebooks available for detailed descriptions should you be planning a trip. Information on all state parks can be obtained by calling (800) 792-1112 or by visiting http://www.wildtexas.com.

Organizations

Today's society is literally overrun with wildlife and environmental organizations of every type. Many of these are well planned, efficiently managed, and based on sound scientific foundations; and many are not. Some organizations are operated with the very best of intentions but with poor results, some are run by lunatics, and a few are complete rip-offs with no real goal other than to reach into somebody's pocket. In the following paragraphs I've listed a few of the organizations that my personal experience has shown to be worthwhile. This certainly doesn't mean that I have anything against every other organization that I haven't mentioned. There are far too many for me even to be familiar with them all, much less list them here. This is just a starting point. The following are simply some of my favorites (as of this writing). They're all doing important work, and most of them can provide a great deal of useful information free or at a nominal charge.

General: National

National Wildlife Federation
    8925 Leesburg Pike
    Vienna, VA 22184

(703) 790-4000
http://www.nwf.org

The Nature Conservancy
International Headquarters
4245 North Fairfax Drive, Suite 100
Arlington Virginia 22203-1606
(703) 841-5300
http://www.tnc.org

National Parks and Conservation Association
1776 Massachusetts Ave, NW
Washington, DC 20036
(800) NAT-PARK
http://www.npca.org

General: Texas

Gulf States Natural Resource Center (NWF Field Office)
4505 Spicewood Springs, Suite 300
Austin, TX 78759
(512) 346-3934

Texas Committee on Natural Resources (NWF Affiliate)
5952 Royal Lane, Suite 168
Dallas, TX 75230
(214) 368-1791

Texas Wildlife Association
1635 NE Loop 410, Suite 108
San Antonio, TX 78209
(210) 826-2904
http://www.texas-wildlife.org

The Nature Conservancy: Texas Field Office
P.O. Box 1440
San Antonio, TX 78295-1440
(210) 224-8774

Specific

The Mule Deer Foundation
1005 Terminal Way, Suite 140
Reno, NV 89502
(888) 375-DEER

Texas Longhorn Breeders Association of America
2315 North Main Street Suite 402
Fort Worth, TX 76106
(817) 625 6241
http://www.tlbaa.org

Horned Lizard Conservation Society
P.O. Box 122
Austin, TX 78796
http://www.hlcs.org

The Peregrine Fund
566 West Flying Hawk Lane
Boise, Idaho 83709
(208) 362-3716
http://www.peregrinefund.org

Texas Ornithological Society
c/o Dr. Keith Arnold
Dept. of Wildlife and Fisheries
Texas A&M University
College Station, Texas 77843-2258
http://www.io.org

American International Rattlesnake Museum
202 San Felipe NW - Suite A
Albuquerque, NM 87104-1426
(505) 242-6569

Bat Conservation International
P.O. Box 162603
Austin, TX 78716
(512) 327-9721
http://www.batcon.org

Bibliography

Author's note: My own experience, opinions, and imagination are usually more than adequate for telling tales around the campfire or down at the local cantina. When it came to writing an actual book, I sometimes needed to draw upon the experience, etc., of others. The following references all played a part in the creation of *Lone Star Menagerie*—some by supplying me with facts and some by resurrecting half-forgotten memories or inspiring me on new courses of research. At any rate, I probably couldn't have written this book without their help, and they deserve to be acknowledged.

Allen, Durward L. *Our Wildlife Legacy*. New York: Funk and Wagnalls, 1954.

Barker, Will. *Wildlife in America's History*. Washington: Robert B. Luce, Inc., 1962.

Barsness, John. "Trouble for Mule Deer." *American Hunter*, Volume 26, Number 7 (July 1998).

Bauer, Erwin A. *Whitetails: Behavior, Ecology, and Conservation*. Stillwater, MN: Voyageur Press, Inc., 1993.

Bedichek, Roy. *Karánkaway Country*. Garden City: Doubleday & Company, Inc., 1950.

Blanchan, Neltje. *Birds*. Garden City: Doubleday, Doran & Company, Inc., 1917.

Bonney, Orin H. "Big Thicket—Biological Crossroads of North America." *The Living Wilderness*, Volume 33, Number 106 (Summer 1969). Washington: US Department of the Interior, 1987.

Brown, David E. *Vampiro: The Vampire Bat in Fact and Fantasy*. Silver City: High-Lonesome Books, 1994.

Davis, William B., and David J. Schmidly. *The Mammals of Texas*. Austin: Texas Parks & Wildlife Department, 1994.

Dobie, J. Frank. *The Longhorns*. Boston: Little, Brown, & Co., 1941.

Doughty, Robin W. *The Mockingbird*. Austin: University of Texas Press, 1988.

_____*Return of the Whooping Crane*. Austin: University of Texas Press, 1989.

Downing, Robert L. "Success Story: White-Tailed Deer." *Restoring America's Wildlife 1937-1987*. Washington: US Department of the Interior, 1987.

George, Uwe. *In the Deserts of This Earth*. New York: Harcourt Brace Jovanovich, Inc., 1977.

Griffin, Donald R. "Sonar in Bats." *Twentieth-Century Bestiary*. New York: Simon and Schuster, Inc., 1955.

Gunter, Pete. *The Big Thicket: a challenge for conservation*. Austin: Jenkins Publishing Co., 1971.

Heymann, M. M. *Reptiles and Amphibians of the American Southwest*. Scottsdale: Doubleshoe Publishers, 1975.

Hillyard, Paul D. *The Book of the Spider: From Arachnophobia to the Love of Spiders*. New York: Random House, 1994.

Jenkinson, Michael. *Beasts Beyond the Fire*. New York: E.P. Dutton, 1980.

Johnsgard, Paul A. *Crane Music: A Natural History of American Cranes*. Washington: Smithsonian Institution Press, 1991.

Laycock, George. *The Alien Animals*. Garden City: The Natural History Press, 1966.

Lemmon, Robert S. *Our Amazing Birds: The Little-Known Facts About Their Private Lives*. New York: Doubleday & Company, Inc., 1951.

Long, Abijah J. and Joe N. *The Big Cave*. Long Beach: Cushman Publications, 1956.

Mason, George F. *Animal Weapons*. New York: William Morrow and Company, 1949.

Meinzer, Wyman. *Coyote*. Lubbock: Texas Tech University Press, 1995

_____*Roadrunner*. Lubbock: Texas Tech University Press, 1993.

Miller, George Oxford. *A Field Guide to Wildlife in Texas and the Southwest*. Austin: Texas Monthly Press, Inc., 1988.

Minton, Sherman A., and Madge Rutherford Minton. *Venomous Reptiles*. New York: Charles Scribner's Sons, 1969.

Page, Lawrence M., and Brooks Burr. *A Field Guide to Freshwater Fishes*. Boston: Houghton Mifflin Company, 1991.

Peterson, Roger Tory. *A Field Guide to the Birds of Texas*. Boston: Houghton Mifflin Company, 1963.

Petrunkevitch, Alexander. "The Spider and the Wasp." *Twentieth-Century Bestiary*. New York: Simon and Schuster, Inc., 1955.

Preston-Mafham, Rod and Ken. *Spiders of the World*. New York: Facts on File, Inc., 1984.

Rouse, John E. *The Criollo: Spanish Cattle in the Americas*. Norman: University of Oklahoma Press, 1977.

Schaefer, Jack. *An American Bestiary*. Boston: Houghton Mifflin Company, 1975.

Schmidly, David J. *The Bats of Texas*. College Station: Texas A&M University Press, 1981.

Sherbrooke, Wade C. *Horned Lizards, Unique Reptiles of Western North America*. Globe: Southwest Parks and Monuments Association, 1981.

Slatta, Richard W. "Life and Death on the Great Trail Drives." *Cowboys & Indians*, Issue 14 (Fall 1996).

Smith, Larry L., and Robin W. Doughty. *The Amazing Armadillo: Geography of a Folk Critter*. Austin: University of Texas Press, 1984.

Solek, Chris. "Mexican Mommas on Maternity Leave." *Enchanted Rock*, Volume 4, Number 7 (September 1997).

Sowls, Lyle K. *The Peccaries*. Tucson: University of Arizona Press, 1984.

Stebbins, Robert C. *A Field Guide to Western Reptiles and Amphibians*. Boston: Houghton Mifflin Company, 1985.

Bibliography

Stoops, Erik D., and Jeffrey L. Martin. *Scorpions and Venomous Insects of the Southwest*. Phoenix: Golden West Publishers, Inc., 1995.

Tuttle, Merlin D. "Saving North America's Beleaguered Bats." *National Geographic*, Volume 188, Number 2 (August 1995).

Van Wormer, Joe. *The World of the Pronghorn*. Philadelphia: J.B. Lippincott Company, 1969.

Walker, Ernest P., et al. *Mammals of the World*. Baltimore: The Johns Hopkins University Press, 1964.

Walker, Stanley. "The Fabulous State of Texas." *National Geographic*, Volume 119, Number 2 (February 1961).

Weidensaul, Scott. *North American Birds of Prey*. New York: Gallery Books, 1989.

Index

Other books from

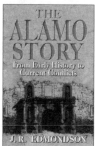

Republic of Texas Press

Return of Assassin John Wilkes Booth

Secrets in the Sky

Southern Fried Spirits: A Guide to Haunted Restaurants, Inns, and Taverns

Spindletop Unwound

Spirits of the Alamo

Spirits of San Antonio and South Texas

Tales of the Guadalupe Mountains

Texas Boys in Gray: Confederate War Letters

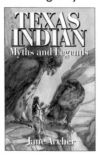

Texas Firehouse Cooks: Favorite Recipes

Texas Golf Guide (2nd Ed.)

Texas Heroes: A Dynasty of Courage

Texas Highway Humor

Texas Indian Myths and Legends

Texas Ranger Johnny Klevenhagen

Texas Ranger Tales

Texas Ranger Tales II

Texas Roadside Restaurants and Cafes

Texas Tales Your Teacher Never Told You

Texas Wit and Wisdom

That Cat Won't Flush

That Terrible Texas Weather

They Don't Have to Die

This Dog'll Really Hunt

Tom Dodge Talks About Texas

Top Texas Chefs: Favorite Recipes

Treasury of Texas Humor

Treasury of Texas Trivia II

Ultimate Chili Cookbook

Uncle Bubba's Chicken Wing Fling

Unsolved Mysteries of the Old West

Unsolved Texas Mysteries

Volunteers in the Texas Revolution: The New Orleans Greys

When Darkness Falls